HULL'S SIDE-FISHING TRAWLING FLEET 1946-1986

Compiled by

MICHAEL THOMPSON

With an Introduction by

Arthur Credland

HUTTON PRESS
1987

Published by the Hutton Press Ltd.
130 Canada Drive, Cherry Burton, Beverley
North Humberside HU17 7SB

Copyright © 1987

First published 1987
Reprinted 1988

No part of this book may be reproduced, stored in a retrieval system or transmitted in any form, or by any means electronic, mechanical, photocopying, recording or otherwise without the prior permission of the Publisher and the Copyright holders

Printed and bound by Clifford Ward & Co.
(Bridlington) Ltd.
55 West Street, Bridlington
East Yorkshire YO15 3DZ

ISBN 0 907033 59 8

Dedication: To my parents, Anne and Harold

ACKNOWLEDGEMENTS

My grateful thanks to Arthur Credland, Keeper of Maritime History, Hull Town Docks Museum, for his most valuable assistance; to Karon Keating of Hull Museums for typing the manuscript; to the staff of the Hull local history library and the technical library, for finding hundreds of reference items; to Adrian Thompson for painting the funnel chart; and to Albert Draper and Son for details of shipbreaking.

Also for the kind use of their photographs:

Aerial Connections
Associated British Ports
Donald Innes Studios
David C. Bell
Grimsby Evening Telegraph
Hull Museums
Kingston Photographers
Malcolm Fussey of Walter Fussey & Son
Memory Lane
Mr. R. Stainthorp
Peter Waugh
S. Hunt (Photographer)

Sources referred to:

Dodd's Comprehensive List of Trawlers
(unpublished typescript)
Fishing News
Lloyds Register of Shipping
Olsen's Fisherman's Almanac
Trawling Times

CONTENTS

INTRODUCTION

THE ORIGINS AND PROGRESS OF THE HULL FISHING INDUSTRY

The story of Hull's fishing industry does not truly begin until the middle of the nineteenth century. Prior to that time any fish caught by vessels sailing out of Hull or brought into the city by fishermen of other ports was entirely for local consumption. A considerable movement around the coast took place from Brixham and other Channel fishing ports to be nearer the huge London market and the rich fishing grounds of the North Sea. A few of the Brixham and Ramsgate smacks began to frequent Scarborough in the summer season, finding a ready sale for their fish to supply the large influx of summer visitors. Some smack owners made their temporary base at Hull bringing their households with them aboard ship at the beginning of the year and returning in the autumn. Hull itself, they soon realised, with a population of some 67,000 people, provided a good outlet for their fish and the rail link established with Leeds in 1840 made it possible to supply it still in reasonably fresh condition to the huge populations of the industrial north. The discovery of the now fabled 'Silver Pits', a prolific source of sole, not far from the mouth of the Humber, was an important factor in the rapid expansion of the Hull fleet from 21 in 1845 to 313 in 1872. Many temporary residents decided to settle here permanently so establishing a solid basis for future development of the fishing trade.

By the 1870's the small single-masted craft had been replaced by the 70-80 ton ketches, or dandy-rigged smacks as they were described locally. Some were built on the south coast in the ports where some of the fishermen had originated but many others were constructed on the Humber or even up the Trent at Burton Stather. To enable fish to be brought quickly to market whilst still fresh the fleeting system was developed by John Sims. The smacks stayed at sea five to twelve weeks at a time off-loading their catch each day, weather permitting, to a fast carrier boat. Before the development of an efficient rail link to London sailing the cutter with its fish packed in ice directly to Billingsgate was the only way to bring the catch in reasonable condition for sale in England's biggest fish market.

The crew of the fishing smacks was small, a skipper, two mates, and two apprentice boys and their job was terrible drudgery. Week after week shooting the nets, hauling, and then transferring the catch in boxes to the cutters by rowing boat. Ice for the boxing fleet was imported from the Norwegian fjords and even in 1920 when there were five ice factories in the city natural ice was still being brought in to satisfy the enormous demand. Arduous work, foul weather and a monotonous diet of fish and potatoes made the smacksmen prey to Dutch 'coopers' selling raw spirits. Disgraceful scenes of drunkenness and maltreatment of the apprentices most notoriously the murder of William Papper by the skipper of the *Rising Sun* in 1881, led to a commission of inquiry into the fishing industry. The danger of the fishermen's life was further emphasised by the great storm of March 1883 when 47 vessels and 260 men were lost. A closer regulation by the Board of Trade and the formation of the Royal National Mission to Deep Sea Fishermen, however, did much to alleviate conditions. The Mission not only gave tracts and encouraged prayer meetings but provided a supply of cheap tobacco which helped wean the men from the hands of the 'coopers' and for the first time provided medical help at sea with a doctor and sick bay aboard the mission vessels.

The smacks were of course dependent on the wind for getting out onto the fishing grounds and needed half a gale to enable them to haul the heavy beam trawl. Steam was introduced onto the cutters speeding up the delivery of fish to the market and this circumstance and the use of paddle tugs to tow the smacks out of Hull to the mouth of the Humber to speed their passage to the North Sea resulted in experiments with auxiliary steam engines. Some of the paddle tugs were themselves converted for fishing and in 1881 Earles Shipyard of Hull launched the first purpose-built steam trawler. Named the *Zodiac* she was built for the Grimsby and North Sea Fishing Co., but the Hull fishing vessel owners realised this was the way ahead and invested in steam with such gusto that within the space of ten years the sailing trawler had vanished from the city. Amongst the leaders of this new age were the Hellyers, a Devon family from Brixham, but the high capital investment needed for the new steam trawlers meant that the industry become concentrated in fewer hands and the days of the owner-skipper had ended.

Another important technological advance was the invention of the otter trawl by Mr. Scott of Granton in 1895. In the old beam trawl the mouth of the net was held open by a stout wooden spar which was limited to a length of not more than fifty feet, beyond which it would tend to sag and buckle. The otter boards, a pair of large iron-bound doors attached to the trawl warps, acted like a pair of wings or hydroplanes which moved outwards under tow keeping the mouth wide open and allowing much larger nets to be used.

The introduction of steam power also enabled trawlers to sail further afield exploiting the grounds off Iceland and Norway and still returning quickly enough for their catch to be in edible condition. These 'single-boaters' fished independently each bringing its catch home packed in layers of crushed ice in the hold. Development of the Icelandic grounds began in 1891 and to achieve this range, a round trip of about 2000 miles, the fish hold had to be filled with coal on the outward journey. Once in Icelandic waters the hold, by then empty of coal, had to be scrubbed clean ready for fish to be stacked.

In the early days the smacks landed their catch near the Victoria Pier and then were grudgingly given a corner of the Humber Dock to find a sheltered mooring for unloading. The completion in 1869 of the West Dock, later renamed Albert Dock, at last gave the opportunity for a coherent development of the trade and the fleet prospered to such an extent that after about ten years there was serious competition for space and it was a great boon when in 1883 St. Andrew's Dock became available. Originally built for an extensive coal trade which never materialised this eleven acre site, practically doubled in extent by the construction of an extension in 1897, remained Hull's fish dock for nearly a hundred years.

The outbreak of the 1914-18 war meant that substantial areas of the home waters were closed to fishing because of the threat of enemy action but the Iceland and Barents Sea grounds remained open. Fleeting in the North Sea ceased for the duration and a large proportion of the British fishing fleet was requisitioned for convoy duties and minesweeping.

After the war ended the Hellyer and Great Northern boxing fleets converted to 'single-boating' while the Red Cross and Gamecock fleets amalgamated and continued in operation until 1936 when declining returns resulted in the company's liquidation. The by now excellent rail communications anyway meant that direct delivery to London by sea was no longer necessary. Over-production was the characteristic feature of the 1930's with falling prices, but the outbreak of the Second World War totally altered the situation. Vessels were requisitioned in huge numbers for war work and most of the traditional fishing grounds were now in the front line for attacks by U-boats, aircraft and surface raiders. By December 1940 only one first-class trawler was landing at Hull but the numbers steadily increased when the government realised what a disastrous loss of a major food resource had taken place. Fishing was organised in convoy with armed protection but because of the dangers of mines and enemy attack many trawlers took their fish into the west coast ports so that for the remainder of the war Fleetwood became the largest British fishing port. After the cessation of hostilities trawlers were gradually returned from their military duties and Hull very soon regained her former crown. Bear Island, Barents Sea and Greenland were favoured at first as these grounds enabled the trawlers to fill their holds quickly and return to port to supply a home market hungry for fish. The Iceland grounds were soon however to regain their pre-eminence and such was the rapid rate of recovery that already in the 1950's the industry was once again witnessing the problems of over-production and falling prices.

Oil-fired trawlers were introduced in 1946 replacing coal with a fuel which was then relatively cheap and much easier and cleaner to handle. The boilers still produced steam which also drove the winches as well as the engines but the first motor trawlers were also appearing on the scene; there were five such in 1955. The post-war period saw the perfection of the traditional side-fishing trawler and some of the finest of these vessels were produced in Yorkshire yards, notably by Cook, Welton and Gemmell at Beverley and their rivals Cochranes of Selby.

Side-fishing had its limitations however, as regards the capacity of the vessel for carrying fish and the ability to return to port whilst the wet cargo was in prime condition. The normal voyage lasted three weeks and beyond that time the fish caught in the early part of the voyage would begin to deteriorate to a significant extent. In addition handling the nets over the side was not an easy process and required a great deal of co-ordinated effort from the crew with constant danger of life and limb. A trawl warp might break under the tremendous strain of hauling and the resultant whiplash could take off a man's arm, leg or head. Fingers were frequently caught in winches and men were lost overboard while trying to bring the net over the side in heavy seas. The answer to all these drawbacks was the stern trawler. Here the trawl was hauled up a stern ramp and the catch dropped down below for processing under cover. The fish was deep frozen so the vessel might stay away for six weeks and more until the hold was full with no risk of deterioration. The first stern-fishing vessel in the Hull fleet was the *Lord Nelson* introduced in 1961. She was in fact a part-freezer storing some of the catch in the traditional way in crushed ice. All the gutting and work previously done on the open deck exposed to all weathers now took place under cover down below and the crew had the unaccustomed luxury of separate cabins and evening film shows. More and larger freezer trawlers were introduced despite the ominous signs of depletion of stocks and the need for effective conservation measures. These were not forthcoming and Iceland made a series of unilateral extensions of her fishing limits. In the Cod Wars of 1958, 1972 and finally 1975 the British fleets were eventually excluded from a zone extending 200 miles around Iceland which effectively meant the end of fishing in the nearest of the 'distant-water' grounds which had been worked continuously by the Hull fishermen since the end of the last century. Limits and quotas were set by Norway and Russia and the home waters were shared out between the various members of the Common Market, so that suddenly there was nowhere for most of Hull's deep-sea fishing fleet to go. The smaller fishing ports with their more limited catching capacity and concentration on near and mid-water fishing fared better but Hull's fishing industry crashed.

Ironically at the same time the Hull trawler owners were deprived of their traditional home — the St. Andrew's Dock had to be vacated to allow the construction of the South Orbital Road. The fleet moved back to Albert Dock where all the vessels remaining in service still have their berths.

This book compiled by Mike Thompson is concerned with the great post-war years of Hull fishing illustrated by a comprehensive collection of photographs of the magnificent side-fishing trawlers. Familiarly known as 'side winders' they reigned supreme until the stern trawlers arrived in the 1960's. The trawl was towed over the starboard side from warps run over a pair of gallows. After a haul the net was brought alongside and the 'bag' hoisted over the deck ready for the mate to loosen the rope holding the cod-end. A cascade of fish poured down into the pounds for the crew ready and waiting with their gutting knives. After washing, the fish was than packed on shelves in the hold between layers of crushed ice. This was a tough life and the men worked to the limits of their endurance sometimes seventeen hours at a stretch on deck, totally exposed to the elements in sub-arctic conditions. There were many disasters, three of the most tragic being the loss of the *Ross Cleveland, Kingston Peridot* and *St. Romanus* in 1968 all within the space of ten days. They were the victims of heavy seas and black ice which formed so thickly on the superstructure their crews were unable to chop it away quickly enough before it caused them to turn turtle. Now there is only one side-fishing trawler operating out of Hull, *Arctic Corsair* of Boyd Line. Built in 1960 at Beverley shipyard she made a series of record catches in 1986 which one hopes is an omen for a new beginning for Hull's once great industry.

ARTHUR G. CREDLAND
Hull Town Docks Museum
June 1987

A set of photographs taken by Peter Waugh on board the "Swanella" (H141) in April 1960.

(Above) The "Swanella" dodging in heavy weather with just enough speed to maintain steerage.

(Right) The Mate releases the cod-end with its protective covering of hides.

(Left) Using the pork line to haul in the belly of the trawl.

(Below) Gutting the fish in the pounds. The flying cod is being thrown into the washer.

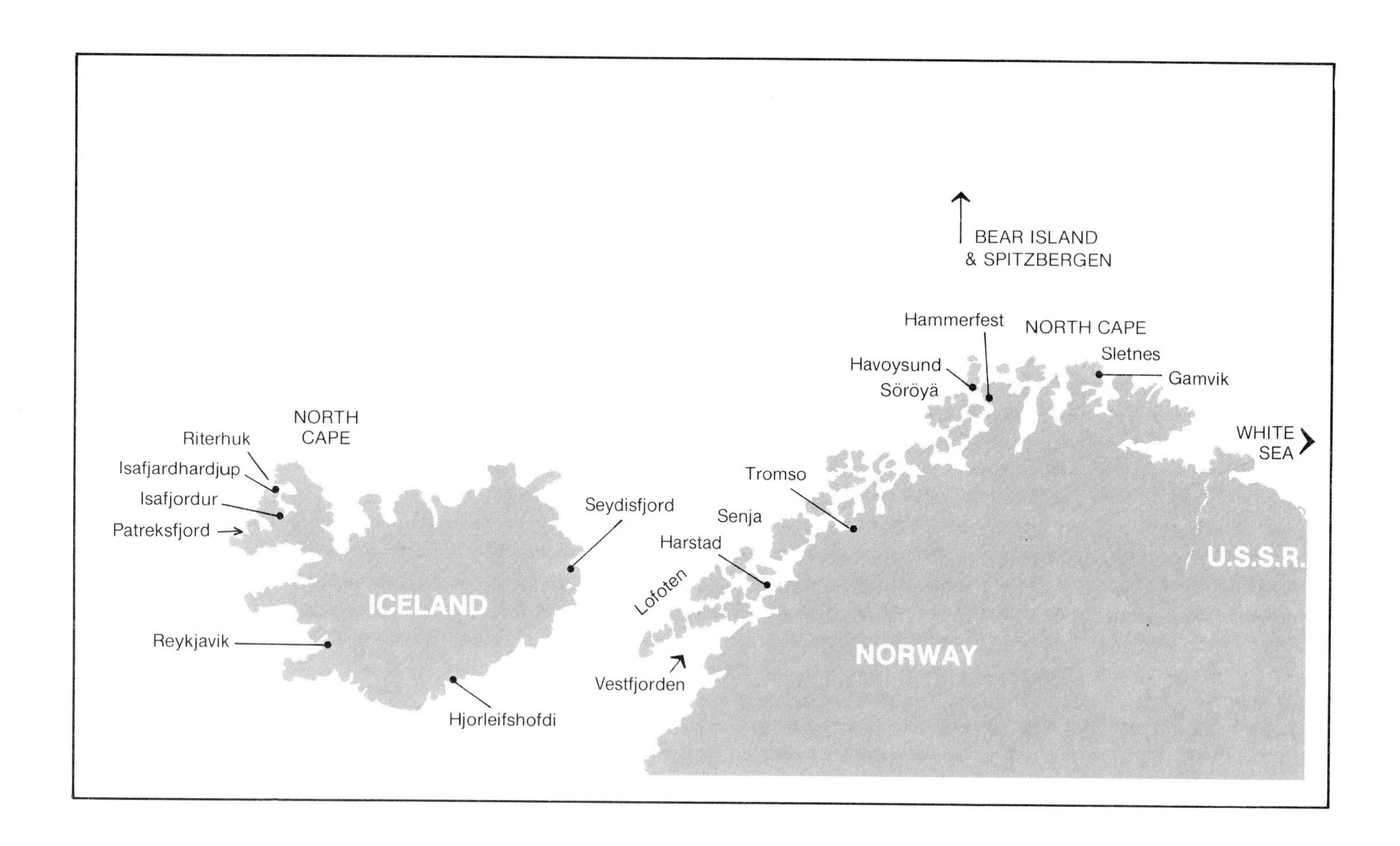
BEAR ISLAND
& SPITZBERGEN
Hammerfest
NORTH CAPE
Sletnes
Havoysund
Gamvik
Söröyä
NORTH
CAPE
Riterhuk
WHITE
SEA
Isafjardhardjup
Tromso
Isafjordur
Seydisfjord
Senja
Patreksfjord
Harstad
U.S.S.R.
Lofoten
ICELAND
Reykjavik
NORWAY
Vestfjorden
Hjorleifshofdi

KEY TO TABLE

Tonnage is shown as follows:

712 = gross tons
262 = net tons

The letters C, O and D after tonnage indicate coal or oil-fired steamers and marine diesel respectively. DE denotes diesel-electric.

Place where vessel was built:

ABD	Aberdeen	GLA	Glasgow	MDL	Middlesbrough
AYR	Ayr	GOO	Goole	REN	Renfrew
BEV	Beverley	KIE	Kiel	SEL	Selby
BRE	Bremen	LOW	Lowestoft	SHL	Shields
		WIV	Wivenhoe		

The date shown after a ship's previous name is the year the ship acquired a new name, e.g.:

Princess Royal
*Dayspring 62 = Dayspring in 1962 became Admiral Nelson
*Admiral Nelson 63 = Admiral Nelson in 1963 became Princess Royal

Length and breadth are in feet and inches.

By far the greatest number of trawlers were built locally by Cook, Welton and Gemmell and their successors at the Beverley Shipyard (closed 1975), and Cochranes of Selby still in production as part of the North British Maritime Group.

BOSTON DEEP SEA FISHERIES

ST. ANDREW'S STEAM FISHING COMPANY LIMITED

Boston Deep Sea Fisheries began as North Sea Trawler Owners in 1885, operating from Boston, Lincs. After 1918 with the Parkes family in control, they moved to Hull and Fleetwood. In 1939 they acquired the St. Andrew's S.F.Co., a Hull company founded in 1897, which they kept alive as a subsidiary company.

From 1946 the Company built up a fleet of new ships which they sold after a year or so and replaced with even more modern ships. They also managed trawlers for owners of small fleets and single ships. In 1951 the three trawlers of Marine S.F.Co. were bought by St. Andrew's S.F.Co. Then in 1954 the firm of F. & T. Ross was taken over. At various times the Boston D.S.F. also had interests in Grimsby, Lowestoft, Milford Haven, France and Canada. The trawlers' names were of Royalty, prominent people, saints or had the Boston prefix.

BOSTON D.S.F.
Funnel — Cherry Red Hull — Black with white line
ST. ANDREW'S S.F.Co.
Funnel — White with black top Hull — Black with white line

Name (* = previous name)	Off.No.	Reg.No.	Built	Tons	Oil/ Diesel	Length Breadth	Other Details	Scrapped
Prince Charles (1)	183412	H 85	BEV 1949	712 262	O	139.4 28.5	Became Cape Duner in 1951 Became Ross Duner in 1965	1968
Prince Charles (2)	185142	H249	SEL 1953	514 184	D	161.1 29.2	Wrecked 23.1.55 but refloated. Became Loch Melfort 1957. To Fleetwood in 1965	1976
Prince Charles (3)	300404	H 77	BEV 1958	691 247	D	180.1 32.9	To Grimsby 1976	1978
Prince Phillip	183387	H 32	BEV 1948	568 206	O	170.0 29.2	To Grimsby 1955 as Hargood. To Hull 1958 H170 Stella Rigel	Lost 21.12.62
Princess Anne	185150	H268	BEV 1953	442 150	D	169.10 29.1	To France 1954 as St. Just II. To Fleetwood 1967 as Wyre Cleaner	1976
Princess Elizabeth (1)	182626	H 86	BEV 1948	568 206	O	170.2 29.2	Became St. Ronan in 1949	Wrecked 12.10.52

Name (* = previous name)	Off.No.	Reg.No.	Built	Tons	Oil/ Diesel	Length Breadth	Other Details	Scrapped
Princess Elizabeth (2)	183449	H135	BEV	810		189.1	Became Roderigo in 1951	
			1950	289	O	32.2		Lost 21.1.55
Princess Elizabeth (3)	185133	H238	SEL	514		161.1	To Australia 1959 as Southern	
			1952	186	D	29.2	Endeavour	Sank 1979
Princess Royal	301628	H183	SEL	453		139.4	To S. Africa 1969	
*Dayspring 62 *Admiral Nelson 63			1960	150	D	28.5		Still reg.
Admiral Nelson	301628	H183	SEL	453		139.4	Became Princess Royal 1963	
*Dayspring 62			1960	213	D	28.5	To S. Africa 1969	Still reg.
Allan Water	181298	H420	BEV	335		149.0	To Holland 1953. To Lowestoft	
			1946	119	D	25.7	1964 as St. David	1980
D. B. Finn	301661	H332	GOO	701		188.0		
			1961	236	D	32.7		Wrecked 1975
Lammermuir	183460	H105	ABD	729		190.7	To Faroes 1956 as Jegvan	
			1950	265	D	32.3	Elias Thomsen	1976
William Wilberforce	301616	H200	BEV	698		179.9	To Grimsby 1969	
			1959	280	D	32.8		1978
Boston Hurricane	181333	H568	SEL	555		171.0	Became Stella Polaris 1949. Became	
			1948	205	O	29.2	Cape Crozier in 1951	1965
Boston Fury	181661	H252	ABD	760		206.4	To Grimsby 1966 as Brandur	
*Boston Fury 55			1950	269	D	32.2		1969
*Fiskanes 65								
Boston Meteor	183433	H114	ABD	386		150.8	To Canada 1951 as Zarbora	
			1950	136	O	25.1		1969
Boston Seafire	181351	H584	BEV	689		181.7	Became Cape Tarifa 1952	
			1948	249	O	30.7	Became Ross Tarifa 1965	1968
Boston Vampire	183416	H 94	ABD	386		150.8	To Canada 1951 as Zarina	
			1949	136	O	25.10		1969
Colwyn Bay	181294	H387	BEV	517		167.7		
*Duncton 45			1942	190	O	28.1		1964
(RN Hills Class)								
St. Bartholomew (1)	180475	H216	SEL	579		177.6	Became Stella Arcturus 1946	
			1946	216	O	30.2	Became Arctic Outlaw 1967	1968

Name (* = previous name)	Off.No.	Reg.No.	Built	Tons	Oil/ Diesel	Length Breadth	Other Details	Scrapped
St. Bartholomew (2)	181332	H516	ABD	613		195.1	Became Arctic Buccaneer 1952	
			1948	232	O	30.2		1972
St. Botolph	180469	H188	BEV	361		148.0	To Cardiff 1946	
			1946	139	O	25.2	To Fleetwood 1958	1963
St. Chad (1)	181344	H575	BEV	689		181.7	Became Stella Polaris 1951	
			1948	249	O	30.7	Became Ross Polaris in 1965	1968
St. Chad (2)	186698	H 20	BEV	575		165.3		
			1956	210	D	30.5		Wrecked 30.3.73
St. Christopher (1)	181337	H573	SEL	555		171.0	Became Tesla 1949. Became	
			1948	205	O	29.2	Stella Carina 1955	1967
St. Christopher (2)	300397	H 88	BEV	603		165.3	To Grimsby 1961. To South Africa	
			1958	213	D	30.5	1971 as Oratava	1983
St. Crispin (1)	181296	H399	BEV	559		170.8	Became Junella 1951	
			1947	202	O	29.2	Became Farnella 1961	1966
St. Crispin (2)	186688	H 86	BEV	536		166.9		
*Reubens 56			1946	201	O	27.8		1965
St. Hubert (1)	183424	H104	ABD	725		195.10	Became Kingston Almandine 1951	
			1950	265	O	30.2		1975
St. Hubert (2)	186740	H142	KIE	568		178.1		
			1950	199	O	28.7		Lost 29.8.60
St. John	180483	H254	BEV	536		166.9	Became Anthony Hope 1946. To Grimsby	
			1946	192	O	27.7	1957 as Aston Villa. First oil burning steam trawler	1965
St. Mark (1)	180477	H218	SEL	579		177.6	Became Cape Trafalgar 1947. Became Auburn	
			1946	216	O	30.2	Wyke 1955. Became Arctic Hunter 1959	1968
St. Mark (2)	181342	H520	ABD	613		180.1	Became Kingston Aquamarine 1952	
			1948	232	O	30.2		Wrecked 1954
St. Mark (3)	186775	H152	KIE	568		180.1		
*Schleswig 57			1950	199	O	30.2		1965
St. Matthew (1)	181267	H284	BEV	536		166.9	To Belgium 1953. Back to Hull 1956 H70.	
			1946	192	O	27.7	To Grimsby 1957 as Wolverhampton Wanderers	1967
St. Matthew (2)	301660	H201	BEV	810		188.8	Became Macbeth 1969	
*Breughel 61			1957	298	O	32.5		1976

Name (* = previous name)	Off.No.	Reg.No.	Built	Tons	Oil/ Diesel	Length Breadth	Other Details	Scrapped
St. Oswald	162899	H335	MDL	427		160.3	To Grimsby 1950 as Woolton	
*Warwickshire 35			1935	160	C	26.7		1957
*Turquoise 46								
St. Peter	186693	H102	BEV	535		166.9		
*Breughel 55			1946	191	O	27.7		1965
St. Stephen	160106	H299	BEV	355		140.4	Became Lady June 1949. To	
*St. Romanus 39			1928	150	C	24.0	Grimsby 1952 as Recepto	1956
*Oak 46								

MANAGED BY BOSTON D.S.F.L.

Name (* = previous name)	Off.No.	Reg.No.	Built	Tons	Oil/ Diesel	Length Breadth	Other Details	Scrapped
Arnold Bennett	162185	H259	SEL	374		156.2	From 1948	
			1930	167	C	24.5		1955
Dunsby	162895	H306	MDL	422		157.0	To Norway 1953 as Findus I	
*Mildenhall 35 *Sapphire 35			1935	156	O	26.7		1971
Hackness	163952	H202	SEL	387		152.8	To Fleetwood 1958	
*Mendip 46			1934	167	C	25.6		1959
*Stella Dorado 48								

The "Dunsby" left Hull for Norway in 1953, where she lasted until 1971.

The "St. Peter" was originally the Belgian vessel, "Breughel".

The "Prince Charles" won the Silver Cod with Skipper B. Wharam in 1960.

"William Wilberforce" was a successful trawler out of both Hull and later Grimsby.

BOYD LINE LIMITED

Founded in 1936 by Thomas Boyd, who had long family connections with the fishing industry and who had managed another family's fleet before forming his own company. In 1937 he built three new distant water ships and by the start of the 1939-45 War, the Company had six trawlers. After the war Thomas Boyd's son Thomas returned from a distinguished war service in the R.N.V.R., to become Managing Director of Boyd Line in 1950 and also Managing Director of Lord Line. In 1963 he left Lord Line to concentrate on running Boyd Line, which by then had a large fleet. The Company is now managed by Thomas Boyd, the founder's grandson, and operates the last Hull deep-water sidewinder the *Arctic Corsair*. The ships' names all have the *Arctic* prefix.

Funnel — Black top, white with two red bands
Hull — Black with red line

Name (* = previous name)	Off.No.	Reg.No.	Built	Tons	Oil/ Diesel	Length Breadth	Other Details	Scrapped
Arctic Adventurer	164991	H381	BEV	565		172.2		
*St. Loman 51			1936	210	O	29.1		1965
Arctic Avenger	186713	H118	BEV	806		188.6		
*Cape Columbia 67			1956	298	O	32.10		1976
Arctic Brigand	186778	H 52	BEV	793		190.2		
*Marbella 65			1955	279	O	32.5		1975
Arctic Buccaneer	181332	H516	ABD	613		177.6		
*St. Bartholomew 52			1948	232	O	30.2		1972
Arctic Cavalier	301635	H204	BEV	764		191.7	Sold to American company 19.3.81 to	
			1960	256	D	33.11	work in the South Pacific	Still reg.
Arctic Corsair	301638	H320	BEV	764		191.7		
			1960	256	D	33.11		Still fishing
Arctic Crusader (1)	162897	H 90	SEL	441		161.0	Became Stella Pegasi 1946. To Grimsby	
*Hendron 39			1935	191	C	26.6	1947 as Mountbatten	1954
Arctic Crusader (2)	163950	H333	SEL	473		161.0	Became Etonian 1952	
*Cape Barfleur 46			1934	188	C	26.6	Became Glenella 1955	1957
*Etonian 50								
Arctic Crusader (3)	183403	H 74	SEL	676		178.4		
*Boynton Wyke 59			1948	268	O	30.7		1969

Name (* = previous name)	Off.No.	Reg.No.	Built	Tons	Oil/ Diesel	Length Breadth	Other Details	Scrapped
Arctic Explorer	165010	H287	SEL	501		166.7	The last pre-war trawler sailing	
*Arctic Explorer 46			1937	187	O	27.6	out of Hull	1967
*Capt. Oates 48								
Arctic Galliard	185114	H209	BEV	790		190.2	Became Arctic Outlaw (2) 1973	
*Kirkella 63			1952	286	O	32.1		1974
Arctic Hunter (1)	160822	H 17	BEV	356		140.2	Became Lord Foyle 1950	
*Capel 39			1929	145	C	24.0		1952
Arctic Hunter (2)	180477	H218	SEL	579		177.6		
*St. Mark 47			1946	216	O	30.2		1968
*Cape Trafalgar 55								
*Auburn Wyke 59								
Arctic Invader	164975	H360	BEV	565		172.2		
*St. Kenan 51			1936	216	O	29.1		1966
Arctic Outlaw	180475	H216	SEL	579		177.6		
*St. Bartholomew 46			1946	216	O	30.2		1968
*Stella Arcturus 67								
Arctic Ranger (1)	165007	H251	SEL	493		166.7	Became Conan Doyle 1951	
			1937	184	O	27.6		1966
Arctic Ranger (2)	300375	H155	BEV	867		192.4		
			1957	316	O	32.11		25.10.76
Arctic Rebel	301645	H219	BEV	606		165.0	Became St. Matthew 1.5.1979	
*Starella 75			1960	207	D	30.5	Stand-by safety vessel	Still reg.
Arctic Rover	137028	H402	BEV	338		140.3	Became Swanland 1952	
*Kings Grey 50			1915	189	C	25.1		1954
Arctic Scout	164915	H143	SEL	494		166.0		
*Cape Aragona 51			1936	192	C	27.6		1957
Arctic Trapper (1)	148815	H567	SEL	324		138.5		
*Alex. Hills 26 *Moy 47			1917	149	C	23.7		1952
*Coral Island 49 *Forbes 50								
Arctic Trapper (2)	165001	H425	SEL	465		161.8	One of Hull's last coalburners	
*Reighton Wyke 59			1937	173	C	27.1		1962
Arctic Vandal	301677	H344	BEV	594		166.5	Became St. Paul 3.5.1979	
			1961	202	D	30.5	Stand-by safety vessel	Still reg.

Name (* = previous name)	Off.No.	Reg.No.	Built	Tons	Oil/ Diesel	Length Breadth	Other Details	Scrapped
Arctic Viking	165649	H452	SEL	533		166.7	Sank during war but raised and rebuilt	
*Arctic Pioneer 46			1937	203	O	27.6	W. Hartlepool 1947	Lost 18.10.61
Arctic Warrior	185086	H176	SEL	712		181.3		
			1951	256	O	31.1		1975

CHARLESON-SMITH TRAWLERS LIMITED

The Company was a joint venture by Charles Hudson and Cecil Smith which started operations in 1938 with a distant water fleet. In 1948 the Company passed to the Ross Group, but they kept Charleson-Smith going as a subsidiary and built up a large fleet over the years. The fleet ended up as part of British United Trawlers, when Ross Group and Associated Fisheries amalgamated in 1969. The ships were named after stars with the prefix *Stella*. On 22nd November 1965 the Ross prefix was adopted, and also the Ross funnel colours.

CHARLESON-SMITH
Funnel — Black top, white with two black bands
Bow emblem — Five pointed white star
ROSS GROUP
Funnel — Black top, grey with green flag containing a white star Hull — Black

Name (* = previous name)	Off.No.	Reg.No.	Built	Tons	Oil/ Diesel	Length Breadth	Other Details	Scrapped
Stella Altair	303839	H279	SEL	677		180.2		
			1963	225	D	32.11		8.4.81
Stella Antares	183439	H123	BEV	661		181.7		
*Alamein 55			1950	239	O	30.7		1968
Stella Aquila	186702	H114	BEV	780		188.7		
			1956	286	O	32.5		1975
Stella Arcturus	180475	H216	SEL	579		177.6	Became Arctic Outlaw 1967	
*St. Bartholomew 46			1946	216	O	30.2		1968

The "Arctic Invader", "Arctic Adventurer", "St. Elstan", "St. Nectan" and "St. Wistan" were all sister ships which lasted nearly 30 years in service.

"Arctic Warrior" was the first winner of the Silver Cod in 1954.

The "Arctic Ranger" appeared in the Yorkshire Television serial, "Snacker", under the name of "Dynasty Neptune".

The "Arctic Vandal" being harassed by an Icelandic gunboat during the last "Cod War".

Name (* = previous name)	Off.No.	Reg.No.	Built	Tons	Oil/ Diesel	Length Breadth	Other Details	Scrapped
Stella Canopus	180482	H244	SEL	579		177.6		
*Northella 48			1946	216	O	30.2		1967
Stella Capella	181281	H358	BEV	504		167.7		
*Inkpen 46			1942	191	O	28.1		1963
(RN Hills Class)								
Stella Carina (1)	181280	H355	BEV	501		167.7	Became Cape Finisterre 1951	
*Yes Tor 46			1942	198	O	28.1	To Grimsby 1952 as Dragoon	1966
(RN Hills Class)								
*Cape Cleveland 47								
Stella Carina (2)	181337	H573	SEL	555		171.0		
*St. Christopher 49			1948	205	O	29.2		1967
*Tesla 55								
Stella Dorado (1)	163952	H202	SEL	387		152.8	Became Hackness 1948. To Fleetwood 1958	
*Mendip 46			1934	167	C	25.6		1959
Stella Dorado (2)	164938	H307	MDL	531		170.7		
*Angle 46 *Laertes 49			1936	195	O	28.0		1960
*Tripoli 55								
Stella Leonis	301641	H322	BEV	775		189.7		
			1960	267	D	33.6		25.11.78
Stella Pegasi (1)	162897	H 90	SEL	441		161.0	To Grimsby 1947	Sank in tow
*Hendren 39			1935	191	C	26.4	as Mountbatten	14.9.1954
*Arctic Crusader 46								
Stella Pegasi (2)	165651	H414	MDL	459		175.5	Became Spurnella 1955	
*Wolborough 46			1937	173	O	27.1		1962
*Lord Ancaster 48								
*Marath 55								
Stella Polaris (1)	164994	H383	SEL	498		169.7	Renamed Cape Campbell 1949	
*Cape Campbell 37			1936	190	O	27.7		1966
Stella Polaris (2)	181333	H568	SEL	555		171.0	Became Cape Crozier 1951	
*Boston Hurricane 49			1948	205	O	29.2		1965
Stella Polaris (3)	181344	H575	BEV	689		181.7	To Grimsby 1967	
*St. Chad 51			1948	249	O	30.7		1968

Name (* = previous name)	Off.No.	Reg.No.	Built	Tons	Oil/ Diesel	Length Breadth	Other Details	Scrapped
Stella Procyon (1)	164953	H162	MDL	462		178.0	Became Carthusian 1948	
*Pict 48			1936	165	C	27.0		1957
Stella Procyon (2)	182649	H184	BEV	590		174.4		
*Thomas Tompion 58			1950	211	O	29.6		1968
Stella Rigel (1)	164919	H 14	SEL	418		152.8	To Grimsby 1955 as Cradock	
*Admiral Drake 38			1936	162	C	25.6		1960
*Stella Canopus 46								
*Cradock 54								
Stella Rigel (2)	183387	H170	BEV	568		170.0		
*Prince Philip 55			1949	266	O	29.2		Lost 21.12.62
*Hargood 58								
Stella Orion (1)	181293	H379	BEV	575		178.1		
*Lancer 46			1943	228	O	30.0		Lost 7.11.55
(RN Military Class)								
Stella Orion (2)	301699	H235	SEL	778		190.1		
			1962	260	D	34.0		6.8.79
Stella Sirius (1)	163180	H165	MDL	413		150.0	Became Loch Torridon 1948	
*Brimnes 46			1934	156	C	26.7	To Fleetwood 1958	1959
Stella Sirius (2)	165009	H163	MDL	455		178.8	To Grimsby 1959 as Bengali	
*Turcoman 48			1937	165	O	27.1		1963
*Bizerta 55								
Stella Sirius (3)	303836	H277	SEL	677		180.2		
			1963	225	D	32.11		7.4.81

MANAGED BY CHARLESON-SMITH

Name (* = previous name)	Off.No.	Reg.No.	Built	Tons	Oil/ Diesel	Length Breadth	Other Details	Scrapped
Brimnes	163180	H165	MDL	413		150.0	Became Stella Sirius 1946	
			1934	156	C	26.7	Became Loch Torridon 1947	1959
Mendip	163952	H202	SEL	387		152.8	Became Stella Dorado 1946	
			1934	167	C	25.6	Became Hackness 1948	1959

Several trawlers were normally built to one design. But the "Stella Aquila" had no sister ship, only the similar "Stella Antares".

The "Stella Leonis" won the Silver Cod in 1963 and 1964 with Skipper R. Waller. She was runner-up twice as "Ross Leonis".

The "Ross Orion" was a top earner and had a good record in the Challenge Shield, being runner-up in 1975 to the stern-trawler, "Hammond Innes".

The "Carthusian" was named after the former pupils of Charter House School who were called "Old Carthusians". Photo by courtesy of Donald Innes Studio.

ETON FISHING CO. LIMITED

The Eton Fishing Company was founded during the 1939-45 War by the Gillard family, who were also fish merchants. The Company was managed by George Gillard until 1959 when it was sold to Boston D.S. Fisheries. The Company had close links with the Ocean Steam Trawling Co. The ships were named after famous schools.

Funnel — Black top, white with a blue diamond outline containing a blue 'E'
Hull — Black

Name (* = previous name)	Off.No.	Reg.No.	Built	Tons	Oil/ Diesel	Length Breadth	Other Details	Scrapped
Carthusian	164953	H162	MDL	462		178.0		
*Pict 48			1936	165	C	27.0		1957
*Stella Procyon 48								
Etonian	163950	H333	SEL	473		161.0	Became Glenella 1955	
*Cape Barfleur 46			1934	188	C	26.6		1957
*Etonian 50								
*Arctic Crusader 52								
Harrovian	163177	H 16	SEL	422		152.1	Became Yorkshire Rose 1948. To	
*Cape Nyemetzki 47			1934	165	C	25.6	Grimsby 1956 as Furious	1959
Reptonian	163166	H363	BEV	409		154.6	To Fleetwood 1952	
*Basque 39 *Istrid 47			1933	174	C	25.6		1959
*St. Arcadius 47								
Rossallian	164399	H164	MDL	432		162.3		
*Lincolnshire 46			1936	157	C	26.7		1957
*Lord Wavell 46								
*Loch Inver 48 *Maxim 48								

THOMAS HAMLING & CO. LIMITED

Established in 1893 the Company began with a North Sea fishing fleet then progressed to distant water trawlers. They were pioneers of fishing at Bear Island. After the 1939-45 War the Company began fishing with several of its pre-war ships which were returned from R.N. service. Then, in 1948, began a programme of building ships at Beverley, which lasted until 1962. The Company lost its fight to keep trading in 1983, its fleet having no viable fishing grounds to work. The ships were named after lesser-known saints.

Funnel — Black top, buff with a wide orange band; a black line separated the buff and orange.
Hull — Black, yellow line

Name (* = previous name)	Off.No.	Reg.No.	Built	Tons	Oil/ Diesel	Length Breadth	Other Details	Scrapped
St. Achilleus	168620	H215	BEV	567		184.10		
*Van Eyck 59 and 64			1951	206	O	29.2		1969
*North Holme 61								
St. Alcuin	183446	H125	BEV	742		199.11		
			1950	271	O	30.8		1974
St. Amandus	163954	H247	MDL	443		162.1		
*Loch Melfort 46			1934	164	C	26.7		Wrecked 1947
St. Amant	183391	H 42	BEV	684		197.10		
*Swanella 52			1949	246	O	30.8		1973
St. Andronicus	305744	H241	BEV	576		185.3		
*Van Orley 64			1951	206	O	29.2		1969
St. Apollo	181359	H592	BEV	658		181.7		
			1948	232	O	30.6		1974
St. Arcadius	168619	H207	BEV	576		184.10		
*Van Oost 64			1951	206	O	29.2		1968
St. Attalus	164018	H167	BEV	417		155.7	Became Onslow 1947	
*Lady Philomena 47			1936	157	C	26.1		1960
St. Britwin	183443	H124	BEV	742		199.11		
			1950	272	O	30.8		1975

Name (* = previous name)	Off.No.	Reg.No.	Built	Tons	Oil/ Diesel	Length Breadth	Other Details	Scrapped
St. Celestin (1)	148458	H192	BEV	352		140.3	Became Lord Portal 1948	
			1925	149	C	24.0		1955
St. Celestin (2)	185129	H233	BEV	790		207.0		
			1952	287	O	32.2		Sank 27.5.56
St. Dominic	300410	H116	BEV	829		189.5		
			1958	302	DE	34.5		1979
St. Elstan	165685	H484	BEV	564		172.2		
			1937	209	O	29.1		1966
St. Gerontius	301682	H350	BEV	659		173.6		
			1962	221	D	32.2		11.10.80
St. Giles	301687	H220	GLA	658		178.8	Sold to Greenpeace 1981 as	
			1962	232	D	32.5	Sea Shepherd II Marine Biology Research	Still reg.
St. Kenan	164975	H360	BEV	565		172.2	Became Arctic Invader 1951	
			1936	210	O	29.1		1966
St. Keverne	183470	H158	BEV	794		205.6		
			1951	286	O	32.2		1974
St. Leger	185089	H178	BEV	794		205.2		
			1951	286	O	32.2		1975
St. Leander	183383	H 19	BEV	658		181.7		
			1949	232	O	30.6		Wrecked 9.1.51
St. Loman (1)	164991	H381	BEV	565		172.2	Became Arctic Adventurer 1951	
			1936	210	O	29.1		1965
St. Loman (2)	300383	H156	BEV	895		193.6	Largest Hull trawler (tons)	
			1957	326	O	33.5		1976
St. Nectan	164996	H441	BEV	565		172.2		
			1937	210	O	29.1		1967
St. Romanus	305741	H223	BEV	600		185.4		
*Van Dyck 64			1950	218	O	29.2		Lost 1968
St. Ronan	182626	H 86	BEV	568		170.2		
*Princess Elizabeth 49			1948	206	O	29.2		Wrecked 12.10.52
St. Wistan	165690	H486	BEV	564		172.2		
			1937	209	O	29.1		1966

Name (* = previous name)	Off.No.	Reg.No.	Built	Tons	Oil/ Diesel	Length Breadth	Other Details	Scrapped
St. Zeno	167090	H255	BEV	608		178.1	Became Banyers 1952	
			1940	207	O	30.0		1966

MANAGED BY T. HAMLINGS & CO.

Name (* = previous name)	Off.No.	Reg.No.	Built	Tons	Oil/ Diesel	Length Breadth	Other Details	Scrapped
Lady Philomena	164018	H167	BEV	417		155.7	Became St. Attalus 1947	
			1936	157	C	26.1	Became Onslow 1948	1960
Leeds United	144005	H172	MDL	405		155.0	Returned to Grimsby 1947	
*Carmarthen Castle 37			1933	153	C	26.4		1962

HELLYER BROTHERS LTD.

In the middle of the nineteenth century, Charles and Robert Hellyer brought their smack up from Brixham. They went into steam trawling in 1888 as Hellyer Steam Fishing Co. Ltd., with a North Sea fleet. In 1913 they pioneered the use of wireless with their ships. In 1919 they became Hellyer Bros Ltd. After the 1939-45 War the Company started to rebuild its fleet, buying a number of ships and having six new trawlers built at Middlesbrough between 1949 and 1959. Some ships were run by a joint company, Northern Fishing Co. Ltd. In 1960 Hellyers became the controlling interest in Kingston S.F. Co. Ltd. Then in 1963 they amalgamated with Associated Fisheries, becoming managers of the remnants of the Lord Line fleet, which they acquired in 1966. In 1969 Hellyer Bros. became the major constituent of British United Trawlers. The ships were named after tribes and Shakespearean characters.

HELLYER BROTHERS: Funnel — Black top, yellow with a blue flag containing a white 'H' (Diesel ships no black top)
NORTHERN FISHING: Funnel — Black top, buff with two red bands
Hull — Grey

Name (* = previous name)	Off.No.	Reg.No.	Built	Tons	Oil/ Diesel	Length Breadth	Other Details	Scrapped
Arab	164942	H293	MDL	579		170.7	Became Loch Seaforth 1947	
			1936	214	O	28.1		1963
Balthazar	181282	H359	BEV	538		167.7	To Grimsby 1952 as Royal Marine	
*Butser 46 (RN Hills Class)			1942	210	O	28.1		1963

The "St. Nectan" was one of seven sister ships built for Hamlings in 1936-37. Two were lost in the War, the "St. Cathan" and the "St. Goran".

The "St. Giles", catcher turned conserver as the "Sea Shepherd". Greenpeace use the "Sea Shepherd" mainly for their anti-whaling activities. She has also been in action against Canadian seal-hunters and in the Japanese porpoise slaughter.

The "St. Gerontius" was the last of the many Hamling trawlers built at Beverley.

The diesel-electric "St. Dominic" was famous for her large funnel.

Name (* = previous name)	Off.No.	Reg.No.	Built	Tons	Oil/ Diesel	Length Breadth	Other Details	Scrapped
Banquo	181349	H582	ABD	604		170.4	To Fleetwood 1967	
*Thornella 54			1948	222	O	29.2		1967
Benvolio	183411	H 22	MDL	722		184.6		
			1949	262	O	31.2		1975
Brutus	183406	H 28	MDL	727		184.6		
			1949	259	O	31.2		1972
Caesar	185131	H226	MDL	830		189.5		
			1952	317	O	32.2		Wrecked 21.4.71
Esquimaux	181271	H297	BEV	619		178.1	Became Dunsley Wyke 1956	
*Coldstreamer 46			1943	234	O	30.0		1967
(RN Military Class)								
Falstaff	300417	H107	MDL	896		194.0		
			1959	323	DE	34.9		31.1.79
Hausa	162063	H262	SEL	355		140.4		
*Cordella 46			1930	139	C	25.0		1954
Imperialist	167050	H 2	MDL	526		175.9	After being in collision she was beached at	
			1939	193	O	28.7	Scarborough 9.10.1959. To Fleetwood 1965	1966
Kelt	165003	H193	MDL	452		178.8	Became Camilla 1954	
			1937	159	C	27.1		1960
Laertes	164938	H307	MDL	531		170.7	Became Tripoli 1949	
*Angle 46			1936	195	O	28.0	Became Stella Dorado 1955	1960
Lorenzo	185140	H230	MDL	830		189.5		
			1952	317	O	32.2		1975
Macbeth (1)	164438	H113	MDL	575		178.8	To Fleetwood 64	
*Ayrshire 46			1938	215	O	28.6		1966
Macbeth (2)	301660	H201	BEV	810		188.8		
*Breughel 61			1957	298	O	32.5		1976
*St. Matthew 69								
Man-O-War	164423	H181	SEL	517		173.2		
			1937	216	O	28.6		1963
Norman	181272	H289	BEV	629		178.5		
*Bombardier 46 (RN Military Class)			1943	242	O	30.0		Lost 4.10.52

The "Othello" built in 1937 was Hull's last coal-burning trawler, continuing until 1963.

Hellyer Brothers' ships were built by Smith's Dock Company, Middlesbrough. They were sturdy and had long lives. The "Lorenzo" was sister to the "Caesar" which was wrecked in 1971.

The "Portia" hauls her gear, under the watchful eyes of a British frigate.

"Falstaff" won the Silver Cod in 1959 with Skipper N. Longthorpe and was twice runner-up.

Name (* = previous name)	Off.No.	Reg.No.	Built	Tons	Oil/ Diesel	Length Breadth	Other Details	Scrapped
Ophelia	161004	H576	BEV	348		140.3		
*Edwardian 48			1931	149	C	24.6		1954
Orsino	161006	H579	BEV	348		140.3		
*Solon 48			1931	148	C	24.6		1954
Othello	164424	H581	SEL	516		173.2	Hull's last coalburner. For her last trip	
*Le Tiger 47 *Regal 48			1937	285	C	28.6	she loaded 234 tons of coal	1963
Pict	164953	H162	MDL	462		178.0	Became Stella Procyon 1948	
			1936	165	C	27.0	Became Carthusian 1948	1957
Portia	186720	H 24	MDL	883		195.8	Hull's first diesel electric trawler	
			1956	318	DE	34.9		1978
Roderigo	183449	H135	BEV	810		189.1		
*Princess Elizabeth 51			1950	289	O	32.2		Lost 21.6.55
Spaniard	181283	H366	BEV	542		167.7		
*Dunkery 46			1942	220	O	28.1		Wrecked 1949
(RN Hills Class)								
Turcoman	165009	H163	MDL	455		178.8	Became Bizerta 1948. Became Stella Sirius	
			1937	165	O	27.1	1955. To Grimsby 1959 as Bengali	1963
Ayrshire	164438	H113	MDL	575		175.8	Became Macbeth 1946	
			1938	215	O	28.6		1966
Capt. Oates	165010	H287	SEL	501		166.7	Became Arctic Explorer again in 1948	
*Arctic Explorer 46			1937	187	O	27.6		1967

HENRIKSEN AND CO. LTD.

Olaf Henriksen started as a skipper with Hellyers in 1915. He formed his own Company in about 1925, his first trawler being *Tervani*. By the start of World War II he had a fleet of four ships. From 1948 the fleet was built up from the three war survivors, with ships bought from other owners. The Company lasted until 1973 when the last two ships were disposed of. All the ships had seven-letter names, some ancient Greek, others of unknown origin.

Funnel — Yellow with a blue Maltese cross; in the centre of the cross was a white circle containing a red crown.
Hull — Black

Name (* = previous name)	Off.No.	Reg.No.	Built	Tons	Oil/ Diesel	Length Breadth	Other Details	Scrapped
Admetus	181295	H395	BEV	624		178.1		
*Sapper 46			1943	279	O	30.0		1966
(RN Military Class)								
*Cape Gloucester 57								
Banyers	167090	H255	BEV	608		178.1		
*St. Zeno 52			1940	207	O	30.0		1967
Brontes	163191	H236	BEV	424		154.6		
			1934	159	C	25.6		1959
Brunham	163943	H 89	MDL	425		160.3		
*Olvina 49			1934	160	C	26.7		1960
Calydon	183471	H253	BEV	787		205.6		
*Northella 56			1951	280	O	32.1		1973
*Gullberg 65								
Camilla	165003	H193	MDL	452		178.8		
*Kelt 54			1937	159	C	27.1		1960
Evander	164425	H272	SEL	516		173.2		
*Fighter 38			1937	285	O	28.6		1966
*Cape Warwick 55								
Larrisa	308549	H266	BEV	729		199.6		
*Jon Forseti 66			1948	283	O	30.1		1968
Miletus	183404	H 75	BEV	684		181.7		
*Starella 59			1949	242	O	30.7		1969

"Admetus" built as the military-class armed trawler, "Sapper", was named after the legendary Greek Prince of Thessaly.

The "Miletus" was named after an ancient Ionian city which had links with Sparta.

Name (* = previous name)	Off.No.	Reg.No.	Built	Tons	Oil/ Diesel	Length Breadth	Other Details	Scrapped
Monimia	160825	H 43	BEV	347		140.3	To Fleetwood 1948	
			1929	156	C	24.6		1957
Tarchon	186739	H141	BEV	823		190.7	Became Rudyard Kipling 1973	
*Swanella 62			1957	297	O	32.5		1974
Tervani	163162	H530	BEV	410		154.6		
*Lorenzo 39 *Nubia 48			1933	175	C	25.6		1959
Victrix	165004	H428	BEV	427		177.0		
			1937	176	O	27.2		1966

HUDSON BROS. (TRAWLERS) LTD.

The Company was founded in 1913 by Tom Hudson, who came from Greenwich to Hull in 1885, and became a fish merchant in 1902. In 1928 it became Hudson Bros., operating a fleet of distant water trawlers. Starting after the 1939-45 War and through the 1950's, the Company bought and sold a large number of ships and had five new ones built. The Company passed to the Ross Group on 5.2.1960 with a fleet of twelve ships. The ships were named after Capes until 22.11.1965 when the Ross prefix was adopted and Ross funnel colours.

Funnel — Black with wide white band.
Hull — Black with white line
Bow emblem — Shield containing a sailing ship
Ross Group funnel — Black top, grey with green flag containing a white star

Name (* = previous name)	Off.No.	Reg.No.	Built	Tons	Oil/ Diesel	Length Breadth	Other Details	Scrapped
Cape Adair	186716	H119	BEV	806		188.6	To Grimsby 1967	
			1956	298	O	32.10		1968
Cape Aragona	164915	H143	SEL	494		166.0	Became Arctic Scout 1951	
			1936	192	C	27.6		1957
Cape Barfleur (1)	164940	H161	SEL	441		156.0	To Grimsby 1949 as Edward East	
*Quantock 46			1936	171	C	26.1		1960

Name (* = previous name)	Off.No.	Reg.No.	Built	Tons	Oil/ Diesel	Length Breadth	Other Details	Scrapped
Cape Barfleur (2)	164954	H213	BEV	449		161.3	To Fleetwood 1954 as Red Falcon	
*Davy 51			1936	171	C	27.2		Lost 1959
Cape Barracouta	162186	H267	BEV	390		151.5	To Fleetwood 1949 as New Prince	
*Leonidas 38			1930	159	C	24.6		1956
Cape Campbell	164994	H383	SEL	498		169.7		
*Cape Campbell 37			1936	190	O	27.7		1966
*Stella Polaris 49								
Cape Canaveral	303823	H267	SEL	659		190.0		
			1963	237	D	33.11		13.7.78
Cape Cleveland (1)	181280	H355	BEV	501		167.7	Became Stella Carina 1947. Became Cape	
*Yes Tor 46			1942	198	O	28.1	Finisterre 1951. To Grimsby 1952 as	
(RN Hills Class)							Dragoon	1966
Cape Cleveland (2)	183398	H 61	ABD	659		178.1		
			1949	237	O	30.1		Lost 4.2.68
Cape Columbia	186713	H118	BEV	806		188.6	Became Arctic Avenger 1967	
			1956	298	O	32.10	First trawler built with bulbous bow	1976
Cape Comorin	164924	H139	BEV	504		166.6	Became Olvina 1955. To S. Africa	
			1936	192	C	27.7	1960 as Lobelia	1968
Cape Conway	164406	H271	MDL	466		164.1	Became Howard 1948	
*Berkshire			1936	168	C	27.1		1958
Cape Crozier	181333	H568	SEL	555		171.0		
*Boston Hurricane 49			1948	205	O	29.2		1965
*Stella Polaris 51								
Cape Duner	183412	H 85	BEV	712		181.7	To Grimsby 1967	
*Prince Charles (1) 51			1949	262	O	30.7		1968
Cape Finisterre	181280	H355	BEV	501		167.7	To Grimsby 1952 as Dragoon	
*Yes Tor 46			1942	198	O	28.1		1966
*Cape Cleveland 47								
*Stella Carina 51								
Cape Gloucester	181295	H395	BEV	624		178.1	Became Admetus 1957	
*Sapper 46			1943	279	O	30.0		1966
(RN Military Class)								

Name (* = previous name)	Off.No.	Reg.No.	Built	Tons	Oil/ Diesel	Length Breadth	Other Details	Scrapped
Cape Kanin	162181	H586	SEL	355		140.2		
*Cape Kanin 46			1930	152	C	24.5		1954
*Davarr Island 48								
Cape Mariato	164979	H364	BEV	497		169.7		
			1936	191	O	27.7		1965
Cape Matapan	149032	H238	SEL	321		150.2	To Aberdeen 1948	Sunk in
			1925	131	C	24.0	To S. Africa 1953	collision 20.4.60
Cape Melville	160872	H150	SEL	343		140.4	Became Loch Alsh 1946	
			1929	136	C	24.0		1956
Cape Nyemetzki	163177	H 16	SEL	422		152.1	Became Harrovian 1947. Became Yorks. Rose	
			1934	165	C	25.6	1948. To Grimsby 1956 as Furious	1959
Cape Otranto	301692	H227	BEV	823		198.1		
			1962	237	DE	34.5		27.9.79
Cape Palliser	164965	H354	SEL	498		169.7		
			1936	198	O	27.7		1963
Cape Pembroke	162202	H502	BEV	409		170.9	Became Frobisher 1947	
*Kopanes 33			1930	164	C	25.1	To Fleetwood 1950	1957
*Grampian 46								
Cape Portland	164967	H357	SEL	497		169.7		
			1936	189	O	27.7		1965
Cape Spartel	183405	H 79	ABD	659		178.4		
			1949	237	O	30.1		1968
Cape Tarifa	181351	H584	BEV	689		181.7	To Grimsby 1967. Lost on Goodwin	
*Boston Seafire 52			1948	249	O	30.7	Sands on way to breakers	1968
Cape Trafalgar (1)	180477	H218	SEL	579		177.6	Became Auburn Wyke 1955	
*St. Mark 47			1946	216	O	30.2	Became Arctic Hunter 1959	1968
Cape Trafalgar (2)	300374	H 59	BEV	787		189.5		
			1957	285	DE	33.10		4.9.78
Cape Warwick	164425	H272	SEL	516		173.2	Became Evander 1955	
*Fighter 38			1937	285	O	28.6		1966
*Compton 39								

"Cape Palliser" and her sister ships, "Cape Portland", "Cape Campbell" and "Cape Mariato" were long-serving ships, but their sister, "Cape Chelyuskin" was sunk in action off Norway in 1940. Photo by courtesy of "Grimsby Evening Telegraph".

"Cape Trafalgar" was runner-up for the Silver Cod in 1961. As "Ross Trafalgar" she won the Challenge Shield in 1972.

(Left) "Cape Columbia" was the first Hull trawler built with a bulbous bow.

(Below left) The "Ross Canaveral" was a successful trawler, but she lasted only 15 years, being scrapped in 1978 due to the industry's problems.

(Below right) H307 was Hull Merchants Amalgamated's "Tripoli" before becoming the "Stella Dorado".

MANAGED BY HUDSON BROS.

Name (* = previous name)	Off.No.	Reg.No.	Built	Tons	Oil/ Diesel	Length Breadth	Other Details	Scrapped
Quantock	164940	H161	SEL	441		156.0	Became Cape Barfleur 1946	
			1936	171	C	26.1	To Grimsby 1949 as Edward East	1960

ROSS GROUP

Name (* = previous name)	Off.No.	Reg.No.	Built	Tons	Oil/ Diesel	Length Breadth	Other Details	Scrapped
Ross Howe	182646	H422	BEV	703		183.5		
*Yardley 65			1950	259	O	31.1		1969
Ross Anson	GY161 Transferred to Hull 1966 until 1967 then back to Grimsby. In February 1967 Ross Anson with skipper Harry Saunderson towed Ross Procyon from Harstad, Norway, to the Humber lightship, a distance of 1,130 miles							
Ross Resolution	GY527 Transferred to Hull 1969 until 1978. Sold to West Indies 28.4.1978							

HULL MERCHANTS AMALGAMATED TRAWLERS

Formed in 1945 by a group of fish merchants. The Company was managed by A. Bailey and J. Balderson. They bought several old trawlers, one ex-naval trawler and one new trawler. In 1955 the Company sold its five remaining ships to Charleson-Smith. The ships were named after W.W.2 North Africa campaigns.

Funnel — Black with two red bands, in between which were two red "T"s joined, forming an "H" for the Tyne Tees and Humber Division Regimental flash.
Hull — Black

Name (* = previous name)	Off.No.	Reg.No.	Built	Tons	Oil/ Diesel	Length Breadth	Other Details	Scrapped
Alamein (1)	149058	H283	BEV	358		140.4	Became Lady Olwen 1949. To Grimsby	
*Lady Beryl 35			1926	153	C	24.0	1952 as Remindo	Lost 1955
*Stella Rigel 45								

Name (* = previous name)	Off.No.	Reg.No.	Built	Tons	Oil/ Diesel	Length Breadth	Other Details	Scrapped
Alamein (2)	183439	H123	BEV	661		181.7	Became Stella Antares 1955	
			1950	239	O	30.7	Became Ross Antares 1965	1968
Bardia	162064	H302	SEL	375		151.5		
*Armana 46			1930	146	C	25.0		1956
Benghazi	144506	H 66	SHL	257		125.3		
*John Bullock 39			1917	106	C	23.2		Wrecked 1947
*Flying Admiral 45								
Bizerta	165009	H163	MDL	455		178.8	Became Stella Sirius 1955	
*Turcoman 48			1937	165	O	27.1	To Grimsby 1959 as Benghali	1963
Derna	127405	H 84	SEL	236		120.0	To S. Africa	
*Dewsland 41			1907	93	C	21.7		Lost 14.9.1954
Marath	165651	H414	MDL	459		175.5	Became Spurnella 1955	
*Wolborough 46			1937	173	O	27.1		1962
*Lord Ancaster 48								
Sollum	181287	H369	BEV	524		167.7	To Grimsby 1949 as Hargood	
*Portsdown 46			1942	195	O	28.1		1964
(RN Hills Class)								
Tobruk	139940	H 14	BEV	246		117.4	To Aberdeen 1950 as G. D. Taylor	
*Wargrey 46			1917	97	C	22.0		1955
Tripoli	164938	H307	MDL	531		170.7	Became Stella Dorado 1955	
*Angle 46 *Laertes 49			1936	195	O	28.1		1960

KINGSTON STEAM TRAWLING CO. LTD.

Formed in 1897 by a number of local shipping interests, notably the shipowner W. A. Massey & Sons Ltd., as a public Company. Before 1914 the ships fished near-water grounds, but after 1918 the Company went over to distant water fishing. After the 1939-45 War the Company resumed fishing with a large fleet of trawlers under Chairman H. W. Hall. Between 1948 and 1960, fifteen new ships were built at Beverley. In 1954 the Loch Fishing Co. Ltd. was acquired in exchange for 40 per cent of Kingston's shares allocated equally to Hamlings, Hellyers and Hudsons. In 1960 control of the Company passed to Hellyer Bros. The ships were named after jewels, then in the 1920's the Kingston prefix was added.

Funnel — Black top, white with red oval, containing three white crowns.
Hull — Black with white line
Bow emblem — Blue shield with three gold crowns

Name (* = previous name)	Off.No.	Reg.No.	Built	Tons	Oil/ Diesel	Length Breadth	Other Details	Scrapped
Kingston Agate	165692	H489	BEV	464		179.0		
			1937	168	O	27.2		1964
Kingston Almandine	183424	H104	ABD	725		195.10		
*St. Hubert 51			1950	265	O	30.2		1975
Kingston Amber (1)	165677	H471	MDL	467		178.10		
			1937	170	C	27.1		1959
Kingston Amber (2)	301651	H326	BEV	785		193.5		
			1960	270	D	33.11		1980
Kingston Andalusite (1)	163177	H133	BEV	416		163.0	Became Milyna 1948	
			1934	168	C	25.9		1956
Kingston Andalusite (2)	183389	H 41	BEV	684		181.7		
*Farnella 52			1949	246	O	30.6		1969
Kingston Aquamarine	181342	H520	ABD	613		180.1		
*St. Mark 52			1948	232	O	30.2		Wrecked 1954
Kingston Beryl	300419	H128	BEV	691		180.3		
			1959	242	D	32.8		27.6.1979

Name (* = previous name)	Off.No.	Reg.No.	Built	Tons	Oil/ Diesel	Length Breadth	Other Details	Scrapped
Kingston Chrysoberyl	163978	H177	BEV	448		160.6		
			1935	174	C	26.6		1955
Kingston Chrysolite	163967	H205	BEV	450		160.6		
			1935	175	C	26.6		1956
Kingston Coral	164021	H242	BEV	433		162.2		
			1936	166	C	26.6		1956
Kingston Crystal	164921	H281	BEV	433		162.2		
			1936	166	C	26.6		1958
Kingston Cyanite	164019	H237	BEV	433		162.2		
			1936	166	C	26.6		1957
Kingston Diamond	167077	H243	BEV	581		178.8	To Fleetwood 1964	
*Lady Madeleine 46			1939	214	O	30.0		1965
Kingston Emerald (1)	165681	H479	BEV	472		177.0	Became Staxton Wyke 1951	
*Lady Hogarth 46			1937	177	C	27.2		Lost 23.8.1959
Kingston Emerald (2)	186671	H 49	BEV	811		205.2		
			1954	288	O	32.1		1976
Kingston Galena	163968	H217	MDL	443		162.1		
*Matabele 47			1935	168	C	26.7		1959
Kingston Garnet	183425	H106	BEV	717		199.11		
			1950	243	O	30.7		1969
Kingston Jade	183465	H149	BEV	794		205.6		
			1951	287	O	32.1		1975
Kingston Jacinth	185106	H198	BEV	794		205.2		
			1952	287	O	32.1		1975
Kingston Olvine	160890	H209	BEV	379		151.2	To Swansea register 1947 as Langland Bay	
			1930	146	C	26.5	but still sailed from Hull	1954
Kingston Onyx (1)	160057	H365	BEV	357		151.5	To Grimsby 1946 as Moorsom	
			1925	151	C	24.0	To Hull 1947 as Westhope	1956
Kingston Onyx (2)	183453	H140	BEV	794		205.6		
			1950	287	O	32.1		1975
Kingston Pearl (1)	164426	H542	MDL	558		188.5	Became Daystar 1958	
*Scottish 45			1937	222	O	28.7	To Fleetwood 1964	1964

Name (* = previous name)	Off.No.	Reg.No.	Built	Tons	Oil/ Diesel	Length Breadth	Other Details	Scrapped
Kingston Pearl (2)	300413	H127	BEV	691		180.3		
			1958	242	D	32.8		19.3.1980
Kingston Peridot (1)	160840	H 55	BEV	356		151.5	To Grimsby 1946 as Stockham	
			1929	137	C	24.0		1954
Kingston Peridot (2)	181356	H591	BEV	658		197.8		
			1948	232	O	30.7		Lost 1968
Kingston Ruby	165678	H477	BEV	472		177.0	Remained a coal burner, one of the last	
*Lady Rosemary 47			1937	177	C	27.2	at Hull in the 1960's	1963
Kingston Sapphire (1)	164319	H206	MDL	443		162.3		
*Cambridgeshire 47			1935	161	C	26.7		1954
Kingston Sapphire (2)	186691	H 95	BEV	809		205.2		
			1955	288	O	32.5		1977
Kingston Sardius	181354	H588	BEV	658		197.8		
			1948	231	O	30.7		1968
Kingston Topaz (1)	160054	H352	BEV	357		151.5	To Grimsby 1946 as Hawkins	
			1927	151	C	24.0		1956
Kingston Topaz (2)	183459	H145	BEV	794		205.6		
			1950	287	O	32.1		1975
Kingston Turquoise (1)	160834	H 45	BEV	356		151.5	To Grimsby 1946 as Cunningham	
			1929	136	C	24.0		1957
Kingston Turquoise (2)	186674	H 50	BEV	811		205.2		
			1955	288	O	32.1		Wrecked 1965
Kingston Zircon	183430	H108	BEV	717		199.11		
			1950	243	O	30.7		1969
Achroite	163935	H 81	BEV	314		133.2	Sold to J. Marr and transferred	
			1934	138	C	24.5	to Fleetwood 1949	Wrecked 1963
Alexandrite	163175	H 7	BEV	313		131.0	Sold to J. Marr and transferred	
			1934	139	C	24.6	to Fleetwood 1949	1963
Almandine	163097	H415	BEV	295		129.0	To Milford Haven 1949	
			1932	135	C	24.0		1963
Andradite	163179	H 26	BEV	313		131.0	Sold to J. Marr and transferred	
			1934	139	C	24.6	to Fleetwood 1949	Wrecked 7.3.1957

The canvas cover on "Kingston Coral" was used to keep the deck cool, by shielding the sun and allowing an air-flow.

The "Kingston Sardius" was the sister ship of the ill-fated "Kingston Peridot".

The ships in "Kingston Jade's" class were the longest side-winders built, at 205 feet. It took three high tides to bring them down the River from Beverley's shipyard.

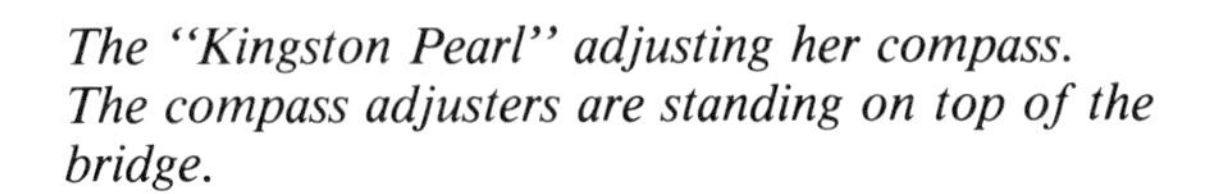

The "Kingston Pearl" adjusting her compass. The compass adjusters are standing on top of the bridge.

Name (* = previous name)	Off.No.	Reg.No.	Built	Tons	Oil/ Diesel	Length Breadth	Other Details	Scrapped
Iolite	180328	H372	BEV	361		136.1	To S. Africa 1953	
*Navena 47			1946	139	O	25.2		Scuttled 1969

MANAGED BY KINGSTON S.T. CO. LIMITED

Name (* = previous name)	Off.No.	Reg.No.	Built	Tons	Oil/ Diesel	Length Breadth	Other Details	Scrapped
Cambridgeshire	164319	H206	MDL	443		162.3	Became Kingston Sapphire 1947	
			1935	161	C	26.7		1954
Euclase	162245	H384	BEV	295		129.0	To Granton 1948	
			1931	131	C	24.0		Lost 22.9.1959
Lady Hogarth	165681	H479	BEV	472		177.0	Became Kingston Emerald 1946	
			1937	177	C	27.2	Became Staxton Wyke 1951	Lost 23.8.1959
Lady Rosemary	165678	H477	BEV	472		177.0	Became Kingston Ruby 1947	
			1937	177	C	27.2		1963
Matabele	163968	H217	MDL	443		162.1	Became Kingston Galena 1947	
			1935	168	C	26.7		1959

LOCH FISHING CO. LTD.

Founded in 1935 by Harry Wight of Aberdeen, the Company began distant-water fishing with a fleet of new trawlers. After the 1939-45 War, the Company received back its ships from the R.N. and they bought several others. Also three new trawlers were built at Aberdeen. In 1954 the Company was taken over equally by Hudsons, Hamlings and Hellyers. They transferred ownership to Kingston S. T. Co. Ltd. in exchange for 40 per cent of Kingston's shares. The Company passed to Hellyer Bros. in 1960, along with Kingstons. The fleet was allowed to keep its identity until the middle 1960's when Hellyers' colours were adopted. The ships were named after Scottish lochs.

Funnel — Black, with black "W" in a white star.
Hull — Green

Name (* = previous name)	Off.No.	Reg.No.	Built	Tons	Oil/ Diesel	Length Breadth	Other Details	Scrapped
Loch Alsh	160872	H150	SEL	343		140.4		
*Cape Melville 46			1929	136	C	24.0		1956
Loch Doon	183422	H101	ABD	670		180.1		
			1949	245	O	30.2		1972
Loch Eriboll	301652	H323	LOW	734		180.8		
			1960	239	D	32.8		9.10.79
Loch Fleet	163963	H569	MDL	443		162.1	To Fleetwood 1958	
*Hausa 39 *Victorian 48			1935	168	C	26.7		1959
Loch Hope	136234	H220	BEV	274		133.5		
*Princess Marie Jose 34			1915	109	C	22.7		Lost 1947
*Feughside 39								
Loch Inver (1)	164399	H164	MDL	432		162.3	Became Rossallian 1948	
*Lincolnshire 46			1936	157	C	26.7		1957
*Maxim 48								
Loch Inver (2)	183442	H110	ABD	670		180.1		
			1950	245	O	30.2		1974
Loch Leven (1)	148957	H186	BEV	357		140.4	Became George Hastings 1948	
			1928	154	C	24.0		1954
Loch Leven (2)	183410	H 82	ABD	670		180.1		
			1949	245	O	30.2		1972

(Above) The "Loch Leven" and her Aberdeen-built sisters were good ships in heavy weather.

(Right) The "Loch Eriboll" was the last trawler built for the Loch Line by Brook Marine of Lowestoft.

Name (* = previous name)	Off.No.	Reg.No.	Built	Tons	Oil/ Diesel	Length Breadth	Other Details	Scrapped
Loch Melfort	185142	H249	SEL	514		161.1	To Fleetwood 1965	
*Prince Charles 57			1953	184	D	29.2		1976
Loch Moidart	181322	H481	SEL	550		180.2	To Fleetwood 1967	
*Murella 51			1947	200	O	29.2		1968
Loch Monteith	164933	H232	MDL	534		170.7		
			1936	195	O	28.1		1964
Loch Oskaig	165657	H431	MDL	534		173.6	Remained a coal burner, one of the	
			1937	198	C	28.6	last at Hull in the 1960's	1963
Loch Seaforth	164942	H293	MDL	579		170.7		
*Arab 47			1936	214	O	28.1		1963
Loch Torridon	163180	H165	MDL	413		157.0	To Fleetwood 1958	
*Brimnes 46			1934	156	C	26.7		1959
*Stella Sirius 48								
Loch Tulla	163933	H225	MDL	424		157.0		
*Reykjanes 39			1934	163	C	26.7		1958

MANAGED BY LOCH F. CO. LIMITED

Name (* = previous name)	Off.No.	Reg.No.	Built	Tons	Oil/ Diesel	Length Breadth	Other Details	Scrapped
Durga	132103	H 83	MDL	216		117.4	To Aberdeen 1948	
			1911	83	C	21.5		1952
Commander Evans	147136	H 20	SEL	344		140.2	To Grimsby 1949 as Tunisian	
			1924	142	C	24.0		1956

LORD LINE

Formed as Pickering and Haldanes S. F. Co. Ltd. in 1888, by Christopher Pickering and Samuel Leeth Haldane. The Company operated a large fleet of near and distant-water ships.

In 1944 the Company was renamed Lord Line and after the war resumed fishing with a big fleet of mainly old ships; then between 1948 and 1951 a large number of trawlers were built at Selby.

In 1950 the Company passed to Associated Fisheries managed by T. W. Boyd, becoming Lord Line Ltd. in 1953. In 1963 Hellyer Bros. amalgamated with Associated Fisheries and in their reorganisation ten ships went to Grimsby under Northern Trawlers. The remainder were managed by Hellyers. In 1966 Lord Line was taken over by Hellyers. The ships were named after Lords.

Funnel — Black top, red with wide white band
Hull — Green with white line

Name (* = previous name)	Off.No.	Reg.No.	Built	Tons	Oil/ Diesel	Length Breadth	Other Details	Scrapped
Lord Alexander	185177	H 12	SEL 1954	790 277	O	183.4 32.0		1975
Lord Ancaster (1) *Wolborough 46	165651	H414	MDL 1937	459 173	O	175.5 27.1	Became Marath 1948. Became Stella Pegasi 1955. Became Spurnella 1955	1962
Lord Ancaster (2)	181350	H583	SEL 1948	636 245	O	177.9 30.8		1967
Lord Ashfield	160838	H 53	SEL 1929	346 135	C	140.3 24.0	To Grimsby 1948 as Calvi	1956
Lord Bann *Bunsen 39 *Jennett 46 *Westheron 50	149045	H465	BEV 1926	357 139	C	140.4 24.0		1952
Lord Beatty	186696	H112	BRE 1956	697 238	O	189.5 31.8	To Grimsby 1963	1976
Lord Cunningham	183396	H 69	SEL 1949	635 243	O	177.9 30.8	To Grimsby 1963	1967
Lord Essendon	164934	H312	SEL 1936	468 201	O	161.3 26.7	To Fleetwood 1964	1966
Lord Foyle *Capel 39 *Arctic Hunter 50	160822	H 17	BEV 1929	356 145	C	140.2 24.0		1952

Name (* = previous name)	Off.No.	Reg.No.	Built	Tons	Oil/ Diesel	Length Breadth	Other Details	Scrapped
Lord Fraser	183392	H 48	SEL	635		177.9	To Grimsby 1948	
			1949	243	O	30.8		1968
Lord Gort	149033	H250	BEV	394		147.5	To Fleetwood 1949 as Wyre General	
*Pict 35 *Elbury 46			1925	174	C	25.1		1956
Lord Grey	160815	H500	SEL	346		140.3	Became Rapier 1948	
			1928	135	C	24.0		1954
Lord Hawke	184313	H 39	ABD	674		180.5	To Grimsby 1963	
*Red Hackle 54			1950	237	O	30.2		1968
Lord Hotham	164927	H231	SEL	466		161.3	To Fleetwood 1963	
			1936	178	O	26.7		1967
Lord Howe	183217	H 19	ABD	674		180.5	To Grimsby 1963	
*Red Rose 54			1950	237	O	30.2		1971
Lord Irwin	160817	H501	SEL	346		140.3		
			1928	135	C	24.0		1954
Lord Jellicoe	301694	H228	BEV	596		166.5	To Grimsby 1963. Now stand-by	
			1962	224	D	30.5	vessel St. Louis	Still reg.
Lord Lloyd	163155	H263	SEL	397		150.5	To Fleetwood 1958	
			1933	151	C	25.6		1963
Lord Lovat	183464	H148	SEL	713		181.3		
			1951	256	O	31.1		10.4.76
Lord Lovel	162291	H506	BRE	266		137.1	To Granton 1952	
*Paul Rykens 48			1935	113	O	24.1		1961
Lord Melchett	163155	H 1	SEL	347		140.3	To Grimsby 1948 as Nelis	
			1929	135	C	24.0		1957
Lord Middleton	164923	H282	SEL	464		161.3	To Fleetwood 1963	
			1936	181	O	26.7		1964
Lord Montgomery	162260	H401	BEV	388		174.5	To Fleetwood 1958	
*Basuto 47			1932	154	O	25.1		1963
Lord Mountevens	183473	H169	SEL	712		181.3	To Grimsby 1963	
			1951	256	O	31.1		1973
Lord Nuffield	183381	H473	SEL	466		161.3	To Fleetwood 1964. The last of the pre-war	
			1937	188	O	26.7	fleet to be scrapped	1967

"Lord Wavell" was the first ship built for Lord Line by Cochranes of Selby in 1948.

A stern view of the "Lord Wavell". All ships in this class had no boat deck.

Built at Selby in 1962, "Lord Jellicoe" and her sister "Lord St. Vincent" were the last ships built for the Lord Line. They are currently sailing as oil-rig tenders.

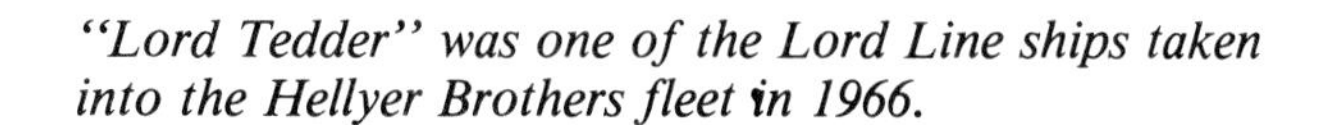

"Lord Tedder" was one of the Lord Line ships taken into the Hellyer Brothers fleet in 1966.

Name (* = previous name)	Off.No.	Reg.No.	Built	Tons	Oil/ Diesel	Length Breadth	Other Details	Scrapped
Lord Plender	163161	H191	SEL	398		150.5	To Fleetwood 1958	
			1933	151	C	25.6		1963
Lord Portal (1)	162264	H406	BEV	402		174.4	Became Vian 1948	
*Negro 46			1932	155	C	25.1		1957
Lord Portal (2)	148458	H192	BEV	352		140.3		
*St. Celestin 48			1925	149	C	24.0		1955
Lord Rivers	162293	H485	BRE	266		127.6	To Granton 1952	
*Peter Hendriks 48			1935	113	O	24.1		1964
Lord Rowallan	183381	H 9	SEL	636		177.9	To Grimsby 1963	
			1949	244	O	30.8		1967
Lord Sands	162292	H503	BRE	266		127.6	To Granton 1952	
*Else Rykens 49			1935	113	O	24.1		1965
Lord Stanhope	163990	H199	SEL	448		157.3	To Fleetwood 1963	Wrecked
			1935	190	O	26.1		Iceland 6.11.63
Lord St. Vincent	303809	H261	BEV	594		166.5	Now stand-by vessel St. Anne	
			1962	202	D	30.5		Still reg.
Lord Tay	164428	H286	BEV	509		173.0		
*Italia Caesar 39			1937	206	O	28.7		1964
*Lady Elsa 50								
Lord Tedder	183469	H154	SEL	722		181.3		
			1951	260	O	31.0		22.5.76
Lord Wavell	181346	H578	SEL	636		177.9	To Grimsby 1963	
			1948	245	O	30.8		1970
Lord Willoughby	183388	H 36	SEL	636		177.9	To Grimsby 1963	
			1949	244	O	30.8		1968

MANAGED BY LORD LINE

Name (* = previous name)	Off.No.	Reg.No.	Built	Tons	Oil/ Diesel	Length Breadth	Other Details	Scrapped
Avola	132884	H382	MDL	255		125.0	To Aberdeen 1947	
*Sasebo 26 *Guyenne 37			1913	99	C	23.5		1954

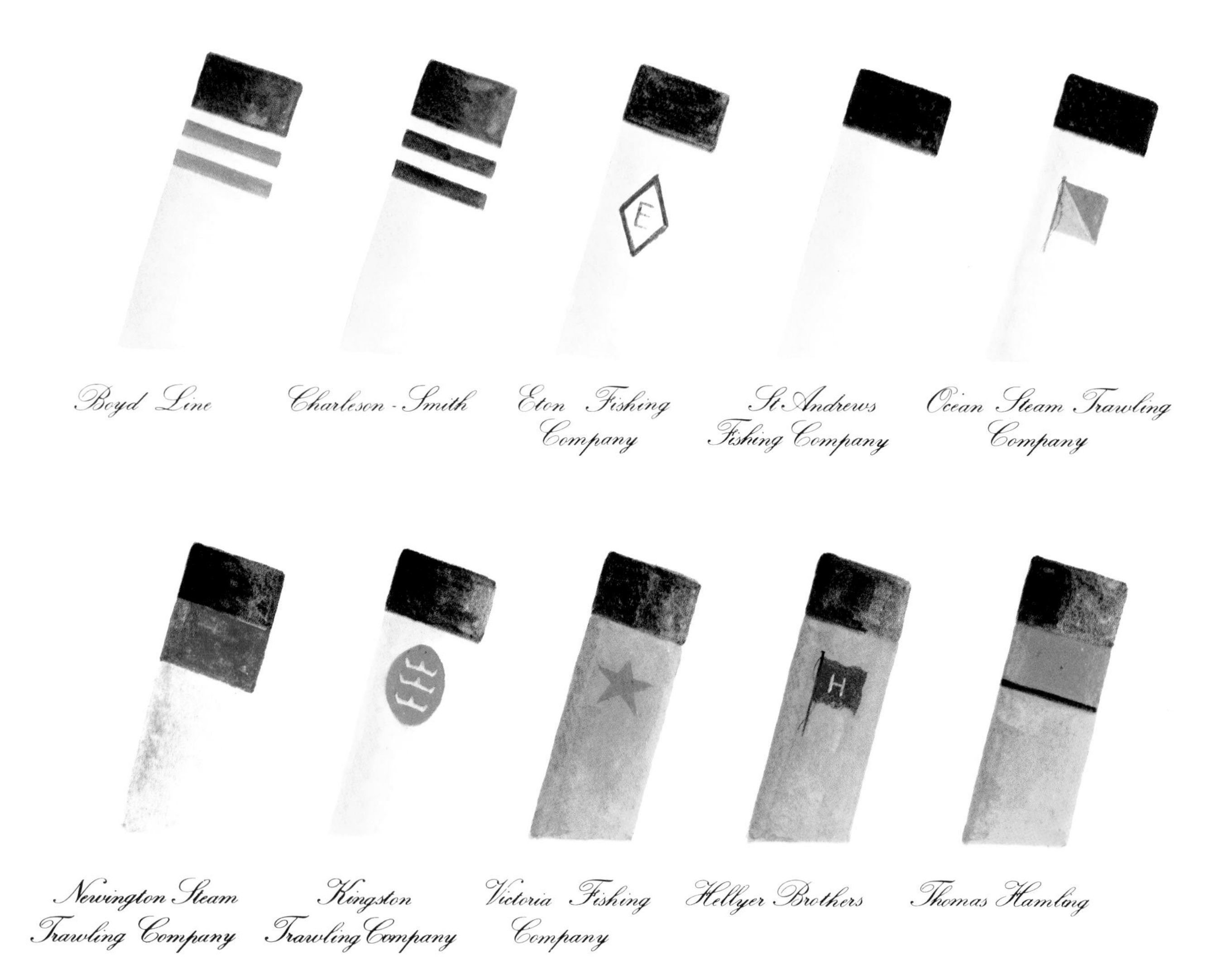
Boyd Line
Charleson-Smith
Eton Fishing Company
St Andrews Fishing Company
Ocean Steam Trawling Company
Newington Steam Trawling Company
Kingston Trawling Company
Victoria Fishing Company
Hellyer Brothers
Thomas Hamling

Hudson Brothers (Trawlers)

West Dock Steam Fishing Company

J. Marr & Son

Loch Steam Fishing Company

Hull Merchants Amalgamated Trawlers

F&T Ross

Henriksen & Company

Lord Line

Ross Group

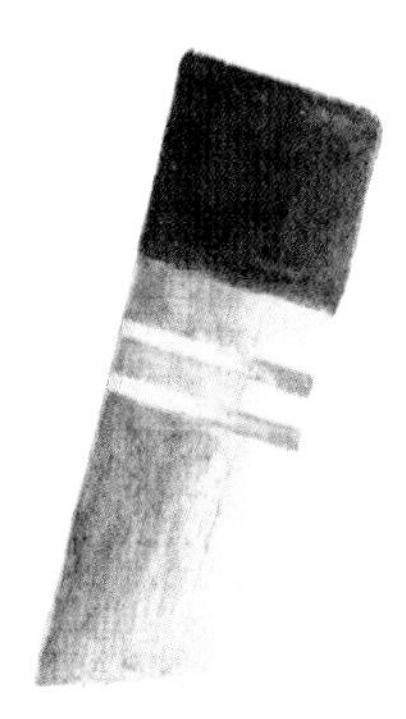

Marine Steam Fishing Company

Name (* = previous name)	Off.No.	Reg.No.	Built	Tons	Oil/ Diesel	Length Breadth	Other Details	Scrapped
Earl Kitchener	136258	H345	BEV	348		140.2		
			1915	162	C	24.1		1953
Cloughstone	125044	H374	SEL	233		117.2	To Milford Haven 1947	
*Argonaut *Ewerby			1907	114	C	22.0		1955
*Jean Max 35								
Mount Ard	162279	H405	ABD	255		121.0	To Aberdeen 1948	
			1931	111	C	22.6		1960
Newland	116118	H653	SEL	235		125.0		
			1903	95	C	21.5		1956
Oystermouth Castle	136112	H378	MDL	283		128.8	To Aberdeen 1949	
			1914	112	C	23.5		1954
Saronta	139956	H390	SEL	316		135.3		
*Vambery 37			1917	127	C	23.5		1952

J. MARR & SON

J. Marr and Son are descendants of Joseph Marr, the Hull merchant and smack owner of the 1870's. In 1902 the Head Office was moved to Hull; also the Hull fleet was expanded by acquiring the Trident S.F. Co. Ltd. and the City S.F. Co. Ltd. From 1946, Chairman Geoffrey Edwards Marr started to build up a large fleet of modern distant-water trawlers for his Hull fleet; also middle-water trawlers for his Fleetwood fleet, some of which often sailed out of Hull. Every few years the fleet was modernised and the older trawlers were sold to other owners. In 1969 the present Chairman, Geoffrey Alan Marr, took over the running of the Company. Although the Company's last sidewinder was sold in 1978, one can still see the small stern-fishers registered at Fleetwood landing at Hull.

The Hull ships' names ended with "ella"; all the others ended in "a."

Funnel — Red with black top
Hull — Yellow with red line

Name (* = previous name)	Off.No.	Reg.No.	Built	Tons	Oil/ Diesel	Length Breadth	Other Details	Scrapped
Bayella	183400	H 72	BEV	580		171.3	In Sept. 1956 Bayella with skipper C. Drever towed the	
*Cayton Bay 52			1949	209	O	29.2	Stella Arcturus home from Spitzbergen	1966

Name (* = previous name)	Off.No.	Reg.No.	Built	Tons	Oil/ Diesel	Length Breadth	Other Details	Scrapped
Benella (1)	183382	H 15	ABD	666		180.5	Became James Barrie 1951	
			1949	235	O	30.1		Wrecked 29.3.69
Benella (2)	300420	H132	BEV	789		189.9	Became Oil Rig Tender 13.2.1978	
			1958	288	D	33.11		Still reg.
Borella	180481	H240	BEV	524		179.5	Sold to S. Africa 1958	
			1946	186	O	27.7		Scuttled 1971
Brucella	185158	H291	BEV	678		175.0		
			1953	248	D	31.7		1977
Carella	163143	H 4	SEL	421		152.1	To Fleetwood 1953	
*Cape Bathurst 36			1933	162	C	25.6		1959
Cordella	181338	H572	ABD	604		170.4		
			1948	222	O	29.2		1965
Farnella (1)	183389	H41	BEV	684		181.7	Became Kingston Andalusite 1952	
			1949	246	O	30.6		1969
Farnella (2)	181296	H399	BEV	559		170.8		
*St. Crispin 51 *Junella 61			1947	202	O	29.3		1966
Glenella	163950	H333	SEL	473		161.0		
*Cape Barfleur 46			1934	188	C	26.6		1957
*Etonian 50								
*Arctic Crusader 52								
*Etonian 55								
Junella (1)	181327	H497	SEL	550		171.0	To Grimsby 1949 as Kirkness	
			1948	200	O	29.2		1964
Junella (2)	181296	H399	BEV	559		170.8	Became Farnella 1961	
*St. Crispin 51			1947	202	O	29.3		1966
Kirkella (1)	164937	H155	SEL	438		157.3	To Grimsby 1952 as St. Benedict	
			1936	172	C	26.1		1960
Kirkella (2)	185114	H209	BEV	790		190.2	Became Arctic Galliard 1963	
			1952	286	O	32.1	Became Arctic Outlaw 1973	1974
Lancella	185151	H290	BEV	790		190.2		
			1953	286	O	32.4		1974
Lorella	181320	H455	BEV	559		170.8		
			1947	202	O	29.2		Lost 26.1.55

Name (* = previous name)	Off.No.	Reg.No.	Built	Tons	Oil/ Diesel	Length Breadth	Other Details	Scrapped
Marbella	186678	H52	BEV	793		190.2	Became Arctic Brigand 1965	
			1955	279	O	32.5		1975
Murella	181322	H481	SEL	550		186.2	Became Loch Moidart 1951	
			1947	200	O	29.2		1968
Northella (1)	180482	H244	SEL	579		177.6	Became Stella Canopus 1948	
			1946	216	O	30.2		1967
Northella (2)	183471	H159	BEV	787		205.6	Became Gullberg (Faroes) 1956	
			1951	280	O	32.1	Became Calydon 1965	1973
Northella (3)	300404	H98	BEV	789		189.8	Became Primella 1963	
			1958	288	D	33.11		1977
Primella (1)	183420	H103	ABD	666		180.5	Became Peter Scott 1957	
			1949	234	O	30.4		1974
Primella (2)	300404	H98	BEV	789		189.8		
*Northella 63			1958	288	D	33.11		1977
Rossella	164997	H336	SEL	498		166.7		
*Hugh Walpole 51			1937	193	C	27.6		1959
Southella	181275	H303	BEV	534		181.2		
			1946	192	O	27.7		1965
Spurnella	165651	H414	MDL	459		175.5		
*Wolborough 46			1937	173	O	27.1		1962
*Lord Ancaster 48								
*Marath 55								
*Stella Pegasi 55								
Starella (1)	183404	H75	BEV	684		181.7	Became Miletus 1959	
			1949	242	O	30.7		1969
Starella (2)	301645	H219	BEV	606		165.0	Became Arctic Rebel 1975	
			1960	207	D	30.5	Became Oil Rig Tender St. Matthew 1.5.1979	Still reg.
Swanella (1)	183391	H42	BEV	684		197.10	Became St. Amant 1952	
			1949	246	O	30.8		1973
Swanella (2)	186739	H141	BEV	823		190.7	Became Tarchon 1962	
			1957	297	O	32.5	Became Rudyard Kipling 1973	1974
Thornella (1)	181349	H582	ABD	604		170.4	Became Banquo 1954	
			1948	222	O	29.2		1967

Name (* = previous name)	Off.No.	Reg.No.	Built	Tons	Oil/ Diesel	Length Breadth	Other Details	Scrapped
Thornella (2)	186686	H84	BEV	793		190.3		
			1955	279	O	32.5		1973
Westella (1)	163176	H349	BEV	426		154.6	To Fleetwood 1957	
*Dervish 35 *Pearl 46			1934	160	C	25.6		1959
Westella (2)	301629	H914	BEV	779		189.7	Sold 1978 to Greenpeace Group named as Sea Shepherd	
			1960	275	D	33.11	Scuttled off Spain 3.1.79 after an incident involving a collision with a pirate whaler	

J. MARR MIDDLE WATER SHIPS REGISTERED AT HULL

Name (* = previous name)	Off.No.	Reg.No.	Built	Tons	Oil/ Diesel	Length Breadth	Other Details	Scrapped
Hildena	185119	H222	BEV	324		135.7		
			1952	117	D	26.7		Capsized 1953
Josena	180473	H207	BEV	341		148.0	To Poland 1947 as Syriusz	
			1946	129	O	25.2		1969
Lucida	187859	H403	BEV	405		149.2	(F.D. 437 Fleetwood Reg. No.)	
			1957	147	D	27.10		1979
Velia	185136	H239	BEV	324		135.7	(F.D. 116 Fleetwood Reg. No.)	
			1952	117	D	26.7		To Italy 1963

MANAGED BY J. MARR & SON

Name (* = previous name)	Off.No.	Reg.No.	Built	Tons	Oil/ Diesel	Length Breadth	Other Details	Scrapped
Alvis	143948	H52	AYR	279		125.2	To Fleetwood 1949	
*Peter Hall			1918	109	C	23.5		1954
*Transport Union 39								
Eastcoates	143925	H393	BEV	277		125.5		
*John Graham 23			1919	108	C	23.5		22.7.55
*Ruby 35								
Clevela	162061	H201	SEL	387		155.5	To Fleetwood 1948 as Red Plume	
			1930	167	C	25.0	To Hull 1955 H83	1955

(Above left) When she was built in 1946 "Northella" was highly acclaimed for her superb design.

(Above right) The "Marbella" was one of four sister ships, the others being "Thornella" and Silver Cod winners, "Lancella" and "Kirkella".

(Left) H141 "Swanella" became Henriksen's top ship "Tarchon". Later as "Rudyard Kipling" she joined her sister ship, "Joseph Conrad", in Newington's fleet.

When "Cayton Bay" was sold to J. Marr in 1952, the "Bay" theme was kept alive by re-naming her "Bayella". Photo by courtesy of Donald Innes Studio.

"Starella" is still sailing as the oil-rig tender "St. Matthew".

Name (* = previous name)	Off.No.	Reg.No.	Built	Tons	Oil/ Diesel	Length Breadth	Other Details	Scrapped
Fyldea	162059	H160	SEL	377		151.5	Became Howard 1947. To Fleetwood	
			1930	149	C	25.0	1948 as Red Dragon	1958

THE MARINE STEAM FISHING CO. LTD.

This was a small Company founded in 1936. The Company bought three ships and named them after bays, i.e. Filey, Runswick and Thornwick Bay. In 1946 they re-formed with two ships and in 1949 built Cayton Bay at Beverley; but in 1951 they sold out to the Boston D.S.F. subsidiary St. Andrew's S.F. Co.

Funnel — Black top, grey with two white bands
Hull — Grey with white line

Name (* = previous name)	Off.No.	Reg.No.	Built	Tons	Oil/ Diesel	Length Breadth	Other Details	Scrapped
Cayton Bay	183400	H72	BEV	580		171.3	Became Bayella 1952	
			1949	209	O	29.2		1966
Colwyn Bay	181294	H387	BEV	517		182.2		
*Duncton 45			1942	190	O	28.1		1964
(RN Hills Class)								
Thornwick Bay	164012	H241	BEV	437		155.7	To Grimsby 1953 as Afridi	
			1936	171	C	26.1		1959

NEWINGTON STEAM TRAWLING CO. LTD.

Founded in 1912 with the trawler *Stanley Weyman*, the Company operated a fleet of around six ships. Under control of the Burton family the Company had great success in the 1960's and early 1970's. They commissioned the first wet fish stern-trawlers *C. S. Forester* in 1969 and *Hammond Innes* in 1973. The ships were named after authors.

Funnel — Black top, grey with a broad blue band
Hull — Black with white line

Name (* = previous name)	Off.No.	Reg.No.	Built	Tons	Oil/ Diesel	Length Breadth	Other Details	Scrapped
Anthony Hope	180483	H254	BEV	536		166.9	To Grimsby 1957 as Aston Villa	
*St. John 46			1946	192	O	27.7		1965
Arnold Bennett	162185	H259	SEL	374		156.2	Sold 1948 to local owners	
			1930	167	C	24.5		1955
Bernard Shaw	160847	H67	SEL	335		150.1	To Denmark 1947 as Hogafossur	
			1929	134	C	24.0		1960
Conan Doyle	165007	H251	SEL	493		166.7		
*Arctic Ranger 51			1937	184	O	27.6		1966
Hugh Walpole	164997	H336	SEL	498		166.7	Became Rossella 1951	
			1937	193	C	27.6		1959
Ian Fleming	308530	H396	BEV	598		193.8		
*Fylkir 66			1958	204	D	32.7		Wrecked 25.12.73
James Barrie (1)	160800	H460	SEL	338		150.0	To Norway 1947 as Nord Rollnes	
			1928	132	O	24.1		1968
James Barrie (2)	183382	H15	ABD	666		180.5		
*Benella 51			1949	235	O	30.4		Wrecked 29.3.69
Joseph Conrad	300386	H161	BEV	823		190.7		
			1958	297	D	32.5		15.10.80
Peter Cheyney	185098	H195	BEV	538		183.3		
*Nolsoyal Pall 51			1947	191	O	29.2		1967
*Faraday 59								
Peter Scott	183420	H103	ABD	666		180.5		
*Primella 57			1949	234	O	30.4		1974
Rudyard Kipling	186739	H141	BEV	823		190.7		
*Swanella 62			1957	297	O	32.5		1974
*Tarchon 73								
Somerset Maugham	301656	H329	BEV	789		189.7		
			1961	275	D	33.11		19.9.78
Warwick Deeping	164006	H151	BEV	420		155.7		
*Lady Beryl 48			1935	156	C	26.1		1959

(Right) In her 30 years of service, H251 spent her first 15 as "Arctic Ranger" and the second 15 as "Conan Doyle".

(Below) Built in 1958. "Joseph Conrad" was the last steam ship built for Hull owners. She was converted to diesel in a Dutch yard in February 1972.

(Above) H141 was re-named "Rudyard Kipling" when 16 years old. She lasted for just over a year longer before survey and repair costs caused her to be scrapped in Spain in 1974.

(Right) The "Vian" was named after Admiral Sir Philip Vian, hero of the Altmark incident in the 1939-45 War. Photo courtesy of Donald Innes Studio.

THE OCEAN STEAM TRAWLING CO. LIMITED

The Ocean Steam Trawling Company was founded just after the 1939-45 War. The fish merchants W. Barkworth and J. Rose were directors. W. Barkworth and then K. Pocklington were managers. The Company closed in 1960. The ships were named after famous seafarers.

Funnel — Black top, white with "O" flag (red and yellow diagonals)
Hull — Black

Name (* = previous name)	Off.No.	Reg.No.	Built	Tons	Oil/ Diesel	Length Breadth	Other Details	Scrapped
Forbes	148815	H567	SEL	324		138.5	Became Arctic Trapper 1950	
*Alex. Hills 20 *Moy 47			1917	149	C	23.7		1952
*Coral Island 49								
Frobisher	162202	H502	BEV	409		170.9	To Fleetwood 1950	
*Kopanes 33			1930	164	C	25.1		1957
*Grampian 46								
*Cape Pembroke 47								
Howard (1)	162059	H160	SEL	377		151.5	To Fleetwood 1948 as Red Dragon	
*Fyldea 47			1930	149	C	25.0		1958
Howard (2)	164406	H271	MDL	466		164.1		
*Berkshire 46			1936	168	C	27.1		1958
*Cape Conway 48								
Onslow	164018	H167	BEV	417		155.7		
*Lady Philomena 47			1936	157	C	26.1		1960
*St. Attalus 48								
Vian	162264	H406	BEV	402		174.4		
*Negro 46			1932	155	C	25.1		1957
*Lord Portal 48								

MANAGED BY THE OCEAN STEAM TRAWLING CO.

Name (* = previous name)	Off.No.	Reg.No.	Built	Tons	Oil/ Diesel	Length Breadth	Other Details	Scrapped
Goth	148478	H211	BEV	394		147.5	To Fleetwood 1948	
			1925	174	C	21.5		Lost Iceland 1948
Norrard	122720	H50	SEL	204		117.0		
*Northward 41			1906	77	C	21.6		1952

F. & T. ROSS LIMITED

The Ross family were shop owners and merchants and eventually became ships chandlers and trawler owners in the 1930's. After 1946 they operated a few ships until 1954 when they were taken over by Boston D.S.F. Ross named their ships after inventors.

Funnel — Black top, red with wide white band which contained a black "R"
Hull — Black

Name (* = previous name)	Off.No.	Reg.No.	Built	Tons	Oil/ Diesel	Length Breadth	Other Details	Scrapped
Davy	164954	H213	BEV	449		161.3	Became Cape Barfleur 1951	
			1936	171	C	27.2	To Fleetwood 1954 as Red Falcon	Lost 1959
Faraday	185098	H195	BEV	538		183.3	Became Peter Cheyney 1959	
*Nolsoyal Pall 51			1947	183	O	29.2		1967
Galvani	160855	H88	BEV	353		140.3	To Fleetwood 1946 as Red Sword	
			1929	138	C	29.2	Returned to Hull 1955 H80	1955
Maxim	164399	H164	MDL	432		162.3	Became Loch Inver 1948	
*Lincolnshire 46			1936	157	C	26.7	Became Rossallian 1948	1957
Tesla	181337	H573	SEL	555		171.0	Became Stella Carina 1955	
*St. Christopher 49			1948	205	O	29.2		1967

(Above) The "Faraday" was originally a Norwegian vessel. She was the last ship to join the F. & T. Ross fleet. Photo by courtesy of Donald Innes Studio.

(Right) The name "Olvina" was an anagram of Skipper Haan's children — Olga, Victor and Nadia.

VICTORIA FISHING CO. LIMITED

Founded in the 1930's by Skipper Haan with the new trawler *Olvina*. The Company owned only three ships yet they lasted until 1960. Ships' names were anagrams of the names of the owner's family.

Funnel — Black top, yellow with a red star
Hull — Black

Name (* = previous name)	Off.No.	Reg.No.	Built	Tons	Oil/ Diesel	Length Breadth	Other Details	Scrapped
Milyna	163177	H133	BEV	416		163.0		
*Kingston Andalusite 48			1934	168	C	25.9		1956
Olvina (1)	163943	H89	MDL	425		160.3	Became Brunham 1949	
			1934	160	C	26.7		1960
Olvina (2)	164924	H139	BEV	504		166.6	To S. Africa 1960 as Lobelia	
*Cape Comorin 55			1936	192	C	27.7		1968

WEST DOCK STEAM FISHING CO. LTD.

The Robins family came to Hull with their fishing smacks from Ramsgate in the 1840's and later went into steam trawlers as J. H. Robins & Co. Ltd., a firm which finished in the 1914-18 War.

The West Dock Steam Fishing Co. Ltd. was founded in 1922 and all the ships were distant-water vessels ending in "Wyke." The fleet was sold in 1954 equally to Boyd Line and Lord Line. But in 1958 the family started a new company, Robins Trawlers Ltd., with two vessels. These were sold in 1961 to Boston D.S.F.

Funnel — Black with wide red band
Hull — Black

Name (* = previous name)	Off.No.	Reg.No.	Built	Tons	Oil/ Diesel	Length Breadth	Other Details	Scrapped
Auburn Wyke	180477	H218	SEL	579		177.6	Became Arctic Hunter in 1959	
*St. Mark 47			1946	216	O	30.2		1968
*Cape Trafalgar 55								

Name (* = previous name)	Off.No.	Reg.No.	Built	Tons	Oil/ Diesel	Length Breadth	Other Details	Scrapped
Boynton Wyke	183403	H74	SEL	676		178.4	Became Arctic Crusader (2) 1959	
			1948	268	O	30.7		1969
Dunsley Wyke	181271	H297	BEV	619		178.1		
*Coldstreamer 46			1943	234	O	30.0		1967
(RN Military Class)								
*Esquimaux 56								
Newby Wyke	183429	H111	SEL	672		178.4		
			1950	253	O	30.7		1975
Reighton Wyke	165001	H425	SEL	465		161.8	Became Arctic Trapper (2) 1959	
			1937	173	C	27.1		1962
Scalby Wyke	163986	H138	SEL	443		156.0		
			1935	173	C	26.1		1959
Staxton Wyke	165681	H479	BEV	472		177.0		
*Lady Hogarth 46			1937	177	C	27.2		Lost 23.8.59
*Kingston Emerald (1) 51								

ROBINS TRAWLERS LTD. (SOLD TO BOSTON D.S.F. 1961)

Name (* = previous name)	Off.No.	Reg.No.	Built	Tons	Oil/ Diesel	Length Breadth	Other Details	Scrapped
Daystar	164426	H542	MDL	558		188.5		
*Scottish 45			1937	222	O	28.7	To Fleetwood 1964	1964
*Kingston Pearl (1) 58								
Dayspring	301628	H183	SEL	414		139.4	Became Admiral Nelson in 1962. Became Princess	
			1960	133	D	28.5	Royal in 1963. Sold to S. Africa in 1963	Still reg.

After the 1939-45 War, some of the old pre-war trawlers were bought by local businessmen and fish merchants. Also a few pre-war trawler owners tried to get re-established. But by the early 1950's, only the larger fleet owners remained.

The following are details of the lesser companies.

The "Newby Wyke" outward bound in the summer of 1960.

H.M.S. "Coldstreamer" was one of 9 military class trawlers built at Beverley in 1943.

H.M.S. "Coldstreamer" as the "Dunsley Wyke".

Hull's long-serving "Darthema" was originally built for Grimsby's famous Cricketer's fleet as the "Larwood". Photo by courtesy of Donald Innes Studio.

ALLIANCE S.F. CO. LTD.

Funnel — White with black top
Hull — Black

Name (* = previous name)	Off.No.	Reg.No.	Built	Tons	Oil/ Diesel	Length Breadth	Other Details	Scrapped
Darthema	160967	H214	SEL	373		155.5	Managed by St. Andrew's S.F. Co. from 1951	
*Larwood 35			1929	161	C	24.0		1954

DAGGER LINE (J. BENNETT, MANAGER)

Funnel — Black top, red with white band
Hull — Black

Name (* = previous name)	Off.No.	Reg.No.	Built	Tons	Oil/ Diesel	Length Breadth	Other Details	Scrapped
Avonwater	162275	H368	ABD	260		124.4	To Aberdeen 1947 as Eileen Paton	
			1930	113	C	23.2		1960
Rapier	160815	H500	SEL	346		140.3		
*Lord Grey 48			1928	135	C	24.0		1954
Yorick	129236	H410	BEV	213		111.4	To Aberdeen 1948	
			1909	87	C	22.6		1956

EASTERN FISHING CO. (1923) LIMITED

Funnel — Black top, buff with two blue bands
Hull — Black

Name (* = previous name)	Off.No.	Reg.No.	Built	Tons	Oil/ Diesel	Length Breadth	Other Details	Scrapped
Commander Holbrook	136225	H223	GOO	227		112.2	To Aberdeen 1949 as Epharatah	
			1915	93	C	22.6		1960
Commander Nasmith	139266	H385	BEV	243		115.5	To Grimsby 1948 as Elmo	
			1915	96	C	22.5		1954

HENDERSONS (Associated with J. Marr & Son)

Funnel — Black top, red with two black bands
Hull — Black

Name (* = previous name)	Off.No.	Reg.No.	Built	Tons	Oil/ Diesel	Length Breadth	Other Details	Scrapped
Fairway	145062	H130	SEL	312		138.5	To Fleetwood 1953	
*Richard Jewell 22			1918	130	C	23.7		1955
*Lord Knaresboro 29								
Lady Enid	144277	H702	SEL	324		138.5	To Fleetwood 1953	
*John Jefferson 20			1918	131	C	23.7		1955
*St. Amant 35 *Lyness 39								

J. C. LLEWELLIN, MILFORD HAVEN (Managed by Boston D.S.F.)

Funnel — White with black top
Hull — Black

Name (* = previous name)	Off.No.	Reg.No.	Built	Tons	Oil/ Diesel	Length Breadth	Other Details	Scrapped
Dalmatia	160113	H474	BEV	360		140.4	Became Westhawk 1948	
*Lady Rosemary 37			1928	142	C	24.0		1953
Jennett	149045	H465	BEV	357		140.4	Became Lord Bann 1946	
*Bunsen 39			1926	139	C	24.0	Became Westheron 1946	1952
Westhawk	160113	H474	BEV	360		140.4		
*Lady Rosemary 37			1928	142	C	24.0		1953
*Dalmatia 48								
Westhaze	160098	H589	BEV	357		151.5		
*Aquamarine 46			1928	151	C	24.0		1955
*Hargood 48								
Westheron	149045	H465	BEV	357		140.4	Became Lord Bann 1946	
*Bunsen 39 *Jennett 46			1926	139	C	24.0		1952

"Westhope" was one of several small company ships managed by Boston D.S.F., whose livery they all carried: white funnel, black top, black hull.

Built in 1902 "Cave" was the oldest trawler fishing out of Hull after the 1939-45 War.

Name (* = previous name)	Off.No.	Reg.No.	Built	Tons	Oil/ Diesel	Length Breadth	Other Details	Scrapped
Westhill	160093	H470	BEV	360		140.4		
*St. Alexander 39 *Larch 46			1928	140	C	24.0		1952
Westhope	160057	H590	BEV	357		151.5		
*Kingston Onyx 46			1927	151	C	24.0		1956
*Moorsom 47								

JUTLAND AMALGAMATED TRAWLERS

Funnel — Black top, white with blue cross
Hull — Black

Name (* = previous name)	Off.No.	Reg.No.	Built	Tons	Oil/ Diesel	Length Breadth	Other Details	Scrapped
Lady Beryl	164006	H151	BEV	420		155.7	Became Warwick Deeping 1948	
			1936	156	C	26.1		1959
Lady Elsa	164428	H286	BEV	509		173.0	Became Lord Tay 1950	
*Italia Caesar 39			1937	206	O	28.7		1964
Lady Madeleine	167077	H243	BEV	581		178.8	Became Kingston Diamond 1946	
			1939	214	O	30.0		1965

OCEAN FISHING COMPANY (SCOTLAND)

Funnel — Black with red ribbon
Hull — Black

Name (* = previous name)	Off.No.	Reg.No.	Built	Tons	Oil/ Diesel	Length Breadth	Other Details	Scrapped
Cave	116085	H643	SEL	247		125.0	The Scottish company sailed Cave out of	
			1902	99	C	21.5	Hull and Grimsby	1950

ODDSSON & CO. LIMITED, HULL

Funnel — Black top, grey with white star
Hull — Black

Name (* = previous name)	Off.No.	Reg.No.	Built	Tons	Oil/ Diesel	Length Breadth	Other Details	Scrapped
Coral Island	148815	H567	SEL	324		138.5	Renamed Arnanes (few months) 1949. Became	
*Alex Hills 26 *Moy 47			1917	149	C	23.7	Forbes 1949. Became Arctic Trapper 1950	1952
Cramond Island	143828	H558	GOO	328		138.5	Renamed Brimnes (few months) 1950	
*John Edmond 46			1918	152	C	23.7	To Aberdeen 1950 as Hetty Milne	1954
Heather Island	163883	H565	REN	339		138.8	Renamed Saudanes (few months) 1949	
			1918	163	C	23.7	To Leith 1949 as Heather Island	1953

K. PERCIVAL (TRAWLERS) LTD., HULL

Funnel — All black, two white bands
Hull — Black

Name (* = previous name)	Off.No.	Reg.No.	Built	Tons	Oil/ Diesel	Length Breadth	Other Details	Scrapped
Sarpedon	139920	H142	BEV	331		135.4	Returned to Grimsby 1948	
			1916	141	C	23.5		1959
Swanland	137028	H402	BEV	338		140.3		
*Kings Grey 50			1915	189	C	25.1		1954
*Arctic Rover 52								

STANDARD S. F. CO.

Funnel — White with black top
Hull — Black

Name (* = previous name)	Off.No.	Reg.No.	Built	Tons	Oil/ Diesel	Length Breadth	Other Details	Scrapped
Silanion	162058	H577	SEL	366		169.2	Became White Flower 1948	
*Dinamar 39			1930	178	C	25.0	Owned by C. Taylor and others	1954

J. TOMLINSON JR.

Funnel — Buff with black top
Hull — Black

Name (* = previous name)	Off.No.	Reg.No.	Built	Tons	Oil/ Diesel	Length Breadth	Other Details	Scrapped
Avondale	143805	H165	WIV	202		115.4		
*William Fall 20			1918	79	C	22.1		1954

UNITED TRAWLERS LIMITED (MILFORD HAVEN)

Funnel — Black with crimson band
Hull — Black

Name (* = previous name)	Off.No.	Reg.No.	Built	Tons	Oil/ Diesel	Length Breadth	Other Details	Scrapped
George Hastings	148957	H186	BEV	357		140.4	From 1950 sailed from west coast ports	
*Loch Leven 48			1928	154	C	24.0		1954

YOLLAND BROS. (MILFORD HAVEN)

Funnel — White with black top
Hull — Black

Name (* = previous name)	Off.No.	Reg.No.	Built	Tons	Oil/ Diesel	Length Breadth	Other Details	Scrapped
Lady Olwen	149058	H283	BEV	358		140.4	To Grimsby 1952 as Remindo	
*Lady Beryl 35			1926	153	C	24.0		Lost 1955
*Stella Rigel 45								
*Alamein 49								
Lady June	160106	H299	BEV	355		140.4	To Grimsby 1952 as Recepto	
*St. Romanus 39 *Oak 46			1928	150	C	24.0		1956
*St. Stephen 49								

YORKSHIRE TRAWLERS LIMITED, HULL

Funnel — Black top, grey with white rose
Hull — Black

Name (* = previous name)	Off.No.	Reg.No.	Built	Tons	Oil/ Diesel	Length Breadth	Other Details	Scrapped
Kings Grey	137028	H402	BEV	338		140.3	Became Arctic Rover 1950	
			1915	189	C	25.1	Became Swanland 1952	1954
Norland	138941	H266	SEL	302		135.3	To Aberdeen 1952 as Viking Alliance	
*Prefect 37			1916	159	C	23.5		1956
Yorkshire Rose	163177	H16	SEL	422		152.1	To Grimsby 1956 as Furious	
*Cape Nyemetzki 47			1934	165	C	25.6		1959
*Harrovian 48								

Bobbers unloading the catch. Photo by courtesy of Associated British Ports, Hull.

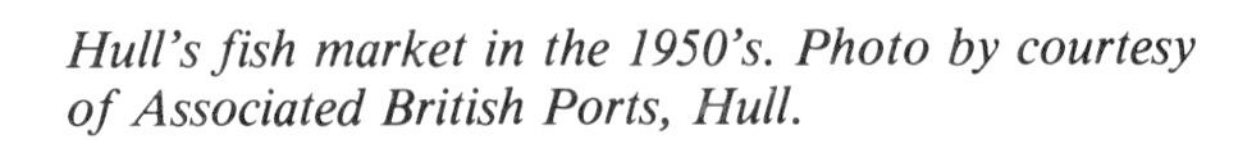

Hull's fish market in the 1950's. Photo by courtesy of Associated British Ports, Hull.

Repair workers, 1956.

INDEX OF HULL REGISTRATION NUMBERS

These were re-allocated when a vessel was scrapped or otherwise ceased fishing; successive trawlers with the same number are recorded in brackets. If a vessel remained at the same port but changed its name there was no alteration to the number. In 1946 there were 136 trawlers on the Hull register, which had increased to 143 ten years later. In 1966 there were 115 sidewinders but the stern-trawler had now made its appearance in the port. A decade after, there were only 36 side-fishing vessels sailing from Hull and in 1986 only one.

1 Lord Melchett
2 Imperialist
4 Carella
7 Alexandrite
9 Lord Rowallan
12 Lord Alexander
14 Tobruk, Stella Rigel 1
15 Benella 1, James Barrie 2
16 Cape Nyemetzki, Harrovian, Yorkshire Rose
17 Arctic Hunter (1), Lord Foyle
19 St. Leander, (Lord Howe)
20 Commander Evans, (St. Chad 2)
22 Benvolio
24 Portia
26 Andradite
28 Brutus
32 Prince Philip
36 Lord Willoughby
39 Lord Hawke
41 Farnella (1), Kingston Andalusite (2)
42 Swanella (1), St. Amant
43 Monamia
45 Kingston Turquoise (1)
48 Lord Fraser
49 Kingston Emerald 2
50 Norrard, (Kingston Turquoise (2))
52 Alvis, (Marbella, Arctic Brigand)
53 Lord Ashfield
55 Kingston Peridot (1)
59 Cape Trafalgar 2, Ross Trafalgar
61 Cape Cleveland 2, Ross Cleveland
66 Benghazi
67 Bernard Shaw
69 Lord Cunningham
70 St. Matthew (1)
72 Cayton Bay, Bayella
74 Boynton Wyke, Arctic Crusader (3)
75 Starella (1), Miletus
77 Princes Charles (3)
79 Cape Spartel, Ross Spartel
80 Red Sword
81 Archroite
82 Loch Leven (2)
83 Durga (Red Plume)
84 Derna, (Thornella (2))
85 Prince Charles (1), Cape Duner, Ross Duner
86 Princess Elizabeth (1), St. Ronan, (St. Crispin (2))
88 Galvani, (St. Christopher (2))
89 Olvina (1), Brunham
90 Arctic Crusader (1), Stella Pegasi (1)

94 Boston Vampire
95 Kingston Sapphire (2)
98 Northella (3), Primella (2)
101 Loch Doon
102 St. Peter
103 Primella (1), Peter Scott
104 St. Hubert (1), Kingston Almandine
105 Lammermuir
106 Kingston Garnet
107 Falstaff
108 Kingston Zircon
110 Loch Inver (2)
111 Newby Wyke
112 Lord Beatty
113 Ayrshire, Macbeth (1)
114 Boston Meteor, (Stella Aquila, Ross Aquila)
116 St. Dominic
118 Cape Columbia, Ross Columbia, Arctic Avenger
119 Cape Adair, Ross Adair
123 Alamein (2), Stella Antares, Ross Antares
124 St. Britwin
125 St. Alcuin
127 Kingston Pearl (2)
128 Kingston Beryl
130 Fairway
132 Benella (2)
133 Kingston Andalusite (1), Milyna
135 Princess Elizabeth (2), Roderigo
138 Scalby Wyke
139 Cape Comorin, Olvina (2)
140 Kingston Onyx (2)
141 Swanella (2), Tarchon, Rudyard Kipling
142 Sarpedon, (St. Hubert (2))
143 Cape Aragona, Arctic Scout
145 Kingston Topaz (2)
148 Lord Lovat
149 Kingston Jade
150 Cape Melville, Loch Alsh
151 Lady Beryl, Warwick Deeping
152 St. Mark (2)
154 Lord Tedder
155 Kirkella (1), (Arctic Ranger (2))
156 St. Loman (2)
158 St. Keverne
159 Northella (2)
160 Fyldea, Howard (1)
161 Quantock, Cape Barfleur (1), (Joseph Conrad)
162 Pict, Stella Procyon (1), Carthusian
163 Turcoman, Bizerta, Stella Sirius (2)
164 Maxim, Loch Inver (1), Rossalian
165 Avondale, (Brimnes (1)), Stella Sirius (1), Loch Torridon)
167 Lady Philomena, St. Attalus, Onslow
169 Lord Mountevans
170 Stella Rigel (2)
172 Leeds United
176 Arctic Warrior
177 Kingston Chrysoberyl
178 St. Leger
181 Man-O-War
183 Dayspring, Admiral Nelson, Princess Royal
184 Stella Procyon (2), Ross Procyon
186 Loch Leven (1), George Hastings
188 St. Botolph
191 Lord Plender
192 St. Celestin (1), Lord Portal (2)
193 Kelt, Camilla
194 Westella (2)
195 Faraday, Peter Cheyney
198 Kingston Jacinth

199 Lord Stanhope
200 William Wilberforce
201 Clevela, (St. Matthew (2), Macbeth (2))
202 Mendip, Stella Dorado (1), Hackness
204 Arctic Cavalier
205 Kingston Chrysolite
206 Cambridgeshire, Kingston Sapphire (1)
207 Josena, (St. Arcadius)
209 Kingston Olivine, (Kirkella (2), Arctic Galliard, Arctic Outlaw (2))
211 Goth
213 Davy, Cape Barfleur (2)
214 Darthema
215 St. Achilleus
216 St. Bartholomew (1), Stella Arcturus, Ross Arcturus, Arctic Outlaw (1)
217 Matabele, Kingston Galena
218 St. Mark (1), Cape Trafalgar (1), Auburn Wyke, Arctic Hunter (2)
219 Starella (2), Arctic Rebel
220 Loch Hope, (St. Giles)
222 Hildina
223 Commander Holbrook, (St. Romanus)
225 Loch Tulla
226 Caesar
227 Cape Otranto, Ross Otranto
228 Lord Jellicoe
230 Lorenzo
231 Lord Hotham
232 Loch Monteith
233 St. Celestin (2)
235 Stella Orion (2), Ross Orion
236 Brontes
237 Kingston Cyanite
238 Cape Matapan, (Princess Elizabeth (3))
239 Velia
240 Borella
241 Thornwick Bay, (St. Andronicus)
242 Kingston Coral
243 Lady Madeleine, Kingston Diamond
244 Northella (1), Stella Canopus, Ross Canopus
247 St. Amandus
249 Prince Charles (2), Loch Melfort
250 Lord Gort
251 Arctic Ranger (1), Conan Doyle
252 Boston Fury
253 Calydon
254 St. John, Anthony Hope
255 St. Zeno, Banyers
259 Arnold Bennett
261 Lord St. Vincent
262 Hausa
263 Lord Lloyd
266 Norland, (Larissa)
267 Cape Barracouta, (Cape Canaveral, Ross Canaveral)
268 Princess Anne
271 Cape Conway, Howard (2)
272 Cape Warwick, Evander
277 Stella Sirius (3), Ross Sirius
279 Stella Altair, Ross Altair
281 Kingston Crystal
282 Lord Middleton
283 Alamein (1), Lady Olwen
284 St. Matthew (1)
286 Lady Elsa, Lord Tay
287 Capt. Oates, Arctic Explorer
289 Norman
290 Lancella
291 Brucella
293 Arab, Loch Seaforth

297 Esquimaux, Dunsley Wyke
299 St. Stephen, Lady June
302 Bardia
303 Southella
306 Dunsby
307 Laertes, Tripoli, Stella Dorado (2)
312 Lord Essendon
320 Arctic Corsair
322 Stella Leonis, Ross Leonis
323 Loch Eriboll
326 Kingston Amber (2)
329 Somerset Maugham
332 D. B. Finn
333 Etonian, Arctic Crusader (2), Glenella
335 St. Oswald
336 Hugh Walpole, Rossella
344 Arctic Vandal
345 Earl Kitchener
349 Westella (1)
350 St. Gerontius
352 Kingston Topaz (1)
354 Cape Palliser
355 Cape Cleveland (1), Cape Finisterre, Stella Carina
357 Cape Portland
358 Stella Capella
359 Baltazar
360 St. Kenan, Arctic Invader
363 Reptonian
364 Cape Mariato
365 Kingston Onyx (1)
366 Spaniard
368 Avonwater
369 Sollum
372 Iolite
374 Cloughstone
378 Oystermouth Castle
379 Stella Orion (1)
381 St. Loman (1), Arctic Adventurer
382 Avola
383 Stella Polaris (1), Cape Campbell
384 Euclase
385 Commander Nasmith
387 Colwyn Bay
390 Saronta
393 Eastcoates
395 Cape Gloucester, Admetus
396 Ian Fleming
399 St. Crispin, Junella (2), Farnella (2)
401 Lord Montgomery
402 Kings Grey, Arctic Rover, Swanland
403 Lucida
405 Mount Ard
406 Lord Portal (1), Vian
410 Yorick
411 St. Nectan
414 Lord Ancaster (1), Marath, Stella Pegasi (2), Spurnella
415 Almandine
420 Allan Water
422 Ross Howe
425 Reighton Wyke, Arctic Trapper (2)
428 Victrix
431 Loch Oskaig
439 Kingston Agate
452 Arctic Viking
455 Lorella
460 James Barrie (1)
465 Jennett, Westheron, Lord Bann
470 Westhill
471 Kingston Amber (1)

473 Lord Nuffield
474 Dalmatia, Westhawk
477 Lady Rosemary, Kingston Ruby
479 Lady Hogarth, Kingston Emerald (1), Staxton Wyke
481 Murella, Loch Moidart
484 St. Elstan
485 Lord Rivers
486 St. Wistan
497 Junella (1)
500 Lord Grey, Rapier
501 Lord Irwin
502 Cape Pembroke, Frobisher
503 Lord Sands
506 Lord Lovel
516 St. Bartholomew (2), Arctic Buccaneer
520 St. Mark (1), Kingston Aquamarine
530 Tervani
542 Kingston Pearl (1), Daystar
558 Cramond Island, Brimnes (2)
565 Heather Island, Saudanes
567 Coral Island, Arnanes, Forbes, Arctic Trapper (1)
568 Boston Hurricane, Stella Polaris (2), Cape Crozier
569 Loch Fleet
572 Cordella
573 St. Christopher (1), Tesla, Stella Carina (2), Ross Carina
575 St. Chad (1), Stella Polaris (3), Ross Polaris
576 Ophelia
577 Silanion, White Flower
578 Lord Wavell
579 Orsino
581 Othello
582 Thornella (1), Banquo
583 Lord Ancaster (2)
584 Boston Seafire, Cape Tarifa, Ross Tarifa
586 Cape Kanin
588 Kingston Sardius
589 Westhaze
590 Westhope
591 Kingston Peridot (2)
592 St. Apollo
643 Cave
653 Newland
702 Lady Enid

THE NUMBER OF SIDEWINDERS REGISTERED AND SAILING OUT OF HULL BETWEEN 1946 AND 1986

Date	Number of Ships
August 1946	136
January 1951	168
January 1956	143
January 1961	140
January 1966	115
January 1971	73
January 1976	36
January 1981	5
January 1986	1

THE ST. ANDREW'S DOCK TUGS

The tugs were owned by the Hull Steam Trawlers' Mutual Insurance & Protection Company.

Name	Built	Scrapped
Bernie	1944	1967
Dagger	1944	1965
Gilder	1944	1964
Kiero	1943	1964
Triune	1943	1965

St. Andrew's Dock in 1966. Photo by courtesy of Associated British Ports, Hull.

St. Andrew's Dock in 1976.

HULL TRAWLERS TRANSFERRED TO OTHER PORTS
TO GRIMSBY

Name	Hull Reg.	Date Transferred	New Name	New Reg.	Scrapped
Kingston Peridot (1)	H55	1946	Stockham	GY89	1954
Kingston Topaz (1)	H352	1946	Hawkins	GY93	1956
Kingston Turquoise (1)	H45	1946	Cunningham	GY86	1957
Leeds United	H172	1947		GY386	1962
Stella Pegasi (1)	H90	1947	Mountbatten	GY477	1954
Lord Ashfield	H53	1948	Calvi	GY576	1956
Lord Melchett	H1	1948	Nelis	GY577	1957
Newland	H653	1948		GY500	1956
Sarpedon	H142	1948		GY466	1959
Commander Nasmith	H385	1948	Elmo	GY241	1954
Commander Evans	H20	1949	Tunisian	GY278	1956
Junella (1)	H479	1949	Kirknes	GY28	1964
Sollum	H369	1949	Hargood	GY8	1964
Cape Barfleur (1)	H161	1949	Edward East	GY16	1960
St. Oswald	H355	1950	Woolton	GY575	1957
Lady June	H299	1952	Recepto	GY254	1956
Cape Finisterre	H355	1952	Dragoon	GY222	1966
Balthazar	H359	1952	Royal Marine	GY213	1963
Kirkella (1)	H155	1952	St. Benedict	GY592	1960
Lady Olwen	H283	1952	Remindo	GY252	Lost 1955
Thornwick Bay	H241	1953	Afridi	GY250	1959
Stella Rigel (1)	H14	1955	Cradock	GY11	1960
Prince Philip	H32	1955	Hargood	GY7	Lost 1962
Yorkshire Rose	H16	1956	Furious	GY20	1959
St. Matthew (1)	H70	1957	Wolves	GY31	1967
Anthony Hope	H254	1957	Aston Villa	GY42	1965
Stella Sirius (2)	H163	1959	Bengali	GY61	1963
St. Christopher (2)	H88	1961	Oratava	GY669	1983
Lord Beatty	H112	1963		GY91	1976
Lord Cunningham	H69	1963		GY109	1967

Name	Hull Reg.	Date Transferred	New Name	New Reg.	Scrapped
Lord Fraser	H48	1963		GY108	1968
Lord Hawke	H39	1963		GY89	1968
Lord Howe	H19	1963		GY82	1971
Lord Jellicoe	H228	1963		GY709	Still reg.
Lord Mountevans	H169	1963		GY79	1973
Lord Rowallan	H9	1963		GY98	1967
Lord Wavell	H578	1963		GY97	1970
Lord Willoughby	H36	1963		GY102	1968
Boston Fury	H252	1966	Brandur	GY111	1969
Ross Adair	H119	1967		*	1968
Ross Duner	H85	1967		*	1968
Ross Polaris	H575	1967		*	1968
Ross Tarifa	H584	1967		*	1968
William Wilberforce	H200	1969		GY140	1978
Prince Charles	H77	1976		*	1978

*Kept Hull Reg. No.

TO FLEETWOOD

Name	Hull Reg.	Date Transferred	New Name	New Reg.	Scrapped
Galvani	H88	1946	Red Sword	LO459	1955
Monimia	H43	1948		FD266	1957
Howard	H160	1948	Red Dragon	LO381	1958
Goth	H211	1948		FD52	Lost 1948
Clevela	H201	1948	Red Plume	LO419	1955
Lord Gort	H250	1948	Wyre General	FD258	1956
Alvis	H52	1949		FD46	1954
Cape Barracouta	H267	1949	New Prince	LO471	1956
Frobisher	H502	1950		LO15	1957
Fairway	H130	1952		FD140	1955
Reptonian	H367	1952		FD171	1959
Lady Enid	H702	1953		FD4	1955
Achroite	H81	1953		*	1963

The "Cape Adair", built in 1956, lasted only 12 years. She was transferred to Grimsby in 1967 as the "Ross Adair", then scrapped in 1968.

"Macbeth" ended her days fishing out of Fleetwood.

The "Cape Matapan" was sold to Aberdeen owners in 1948. She went to South Africa in 1953 and was sunk in 1960 at the age of 35.

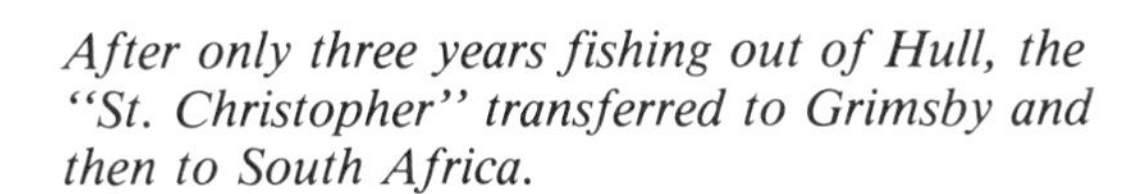
After only three years fishing out of Hull, the "St. Christopher" transferred to Grimsby and then to South Africa.

Name	Hull Reg.	Date Transferred	New Name	New Reg.	Scrapped
Alexandrite	H7	1953		*	1963
Andradite	H26	1953		*	Lost 1957
Carella	H4	1953		FD319	1959
Hildina	H222	1953		*	Lost 1953
Cape Barfleur (2)	H213	1954	Red Falcon	LO4	Lost 1959
Westella (1)	H349	1957		FD318	1959
Hackness	H202	1958		FD120	1959
Lord Montgomery	H401	1958		FD13	1963
Lord Plender	H191	1958		FD59	1963
Loch Fleet	H569	1958		FD43	1959
Loch Torridon	H165	1958		FD44	1959
Tervani	H530	1958		FD61	1959
Onslow	H167	1958		FD50	1960
Lord Middleton	H282	1963		FD67	1964
Lord Stanhope	H199	1963		*	Lost 1963
Lord Hotham	H231	1963		FD64	1966
Daystar	H542	1964		*	1964
Lord Essendon	H312	1964		FD75	1966
Lord Nuffield	H473	1964		FD88	1967
Macbeth	H113	1964		FD74	1966
Kingston Diamond	H243	1964		FD84	1965
Imperialist	H2	1965		FD83	1966
Loch Melfort	H249	1965		FD228	1976
Loch Moidart	H481	1967		FD97	1968
Banquo	H582	1967		FD99	1967

* Kept Hull Reg. No. LO registered London but sailing from Fleetwood

TO SCOTLAND

Name	Hull Reg.	Date Transferred	New Name	New Reg.	Scrapped
Avola	H382	1947		A510	1954
Avonwater	H368	1947	Eileen Paton	GW22	1960
Durga	H83	1948		A458	1952
Yorick	H410	1948		A247	1956

Name	Hull Reg.	Date Transferred	New Name	New Reg.	Scrapped
Mount Ard	H405	1948		A477	1960
Euclase	H384	1948		GN51	Lost 1955
Cape Matapan	H238	1948		A80	Lost 1960
Commander Holbrook	H223	1949	Epharatah	A659	1960
Oystermouth Castle	H378	1949		GW23	1954
Saudanes	H565	1949	Heather Island	LH43	1953
Brimnes	H558	1950	Hetty Milne	A648	1954
Tobruk	H14	1950	G. D. Taylor	A644	1955
Norland	H266	1950	Viking Alliance	A643	1956
Lord Lovel	H506	1952		GN2	1961
Lord Sands	H503	1952		GN3	1965
Lord Rivers	H485	1952		GN4	1964

A = Aberdeen, LH = Leith, GN = Granton, GW = Glasgow (but sailing out of Aberdeen)

TO WALES

Name	Hull Reg.	Date Transferred	New Name	New Reg.	Scrapped
CARDIFF					
St. Botolph	H188	1946		CF8	1963
SWANSEA					
Kingston Olvine	H209	1947	Langland Bay	SA72	1954
MILFORD HAVEN					
Cloughstone	H374	1947			1955
Almandine	H415	1949			1963

TRANSFERRED OUT OF U.K.

Name	Hull Reg.	Date Transferred	New Name	New Reg.	Scrapped
AUSTRALIA					
Princess Elizabeth (3)	H238	1959	Southern Endeavour		Sank 1979
BELGIUM					
St. Matthew (1)	H284	1953	Back to Hull 1956		1967

Name	Hull Reg.	Date Transferred	New Name	New Reg.	Scrapped
CANADA					
Boston Meteor	H114	1951	Zarbara		1969
Boston Vampire	H94	1951	Zarina		1969
DENMARK					
Bernard Shaw	H57	1947	Hogafossur		1960
FAROES					
Lammermuir	H105	1956	Jeguan Elias Thomsen		1976
Northella (2)	H159	1956	Gullberg. Back to Hull 1965		1973
FRANCE					
Princess Anne	H268	1954	St. Just II. Back to Fleetwood 1967 as Wyre General		1976
HOLLAND					
Allan Water	H420	1953	Back to Lowestoft 1964 as St. David		1980
NORWAY					
James Barrie (1)	H460	1947	Nord Rollnes		1968
Dunsby	H306	1953	Findus 1		1971
POLAND					
Josena	H207	1947	Syriusz		1969
SOUTH AFRICA					
Cape Matapan	H238	1953			Lost 1960
Derna	H84	1953			Lost 1954
Iolite	H372	1953			1969
Borella	H240	1958			1971
Olvina	H139	1960	Lobelia		1968
Princess Royal	H183	1969			Still reg.
St. Christopher (2)	H88	1971	Oratava		1983

HULL TRAWLERS LOST OR WRECKED 1946-1986

Due to the hazardous nature of their work it was inevitable that trawler losses would occur. Apart from the ships that sank, numerous others went aground or were in collision, but after repairs they were usually able to return to sea.

It is worth noting the superb rescue work carried out over the years by the R.N.L.I. Lifeboat crewmen, also the Icelandic and Norwegian Coastguard Services.

After suffering the ordeal of being shipwrecked on foreign shores, the crew had to wait for a berth in a homeward-bound trawler or a mailboat, before they could return home. This treatment left many of the survivors and their families with bitter feelings against the owners involved.

Loch Hope H220: Lost 11.6.1947 off East Iceland when a mine which had caught in the nets exploded, causing serious damage to the ship which sank. Eight crewmen were injured and one killed.

St. Amandus H247: Wrecked 24.12.1947 at Skrova in Vestfjord near the Lofoten Islands, Norway, during gales. Also *Pict* and *Stella Orion* ran aground within a few days of each other, but they were re-floated — all crew saved.

Sargon G.Y.858: Wrecked 1.12.1948 at Patreksfjord N.W. Iceland, at night while making for shelter in a blizzard and severe gale. Next morning six men were saved by being hauled up the high cliffs by Icelandic rescue teams in atrocious conditions. But 10 men died from exposure and one was lost overboard. The *Sargon* was a Grimsby ship but she was sailing out of Hull, managed by St. Andrew's S.F. Co. Ltd., and 16 of the crew were Hull men.

Spaniard H366: Wrecked 22.3.1949 off Sletnes Lighthouse, near Gamvik, Finnmark, North Norway. All the crew were saved.

St. Leander H19: Lost 9.1.1951 in the Humber. Whilst manouvering off St. Andrew's Dock the *St. Leander* collided with the *Davy* which was at anchor. She then drifted up to Barton Ness and was taken in tow, but she grounded at Hessle Flats. *St. Leander* was a new ship but unfortunately could not be salvaged and the wreck was blown up. All the crew were saved.

Norman H289: Wrecked 4.10.1952 on Skerries East of Cape Farewell, South Greenland, in thick fog. As the ship listed the crew tried to swim ashore. Twenty men were lost, only one man was saved (by coincidence his name happened to be Norman).

St. Ronan H86: Wrecked 12.10.1952 at St. John's Point, Caithness, Scotland, whilst outward bound for Greenland. All the crew were saved.

Hildina H222: Lost 1.12.1952. Capsized in rough seas north of Scotland, after the trawl had caught fast on the seabed. She had just transferred to Fleetwood; five crewmen were lost.

Kingston Aquamarine H520: Wrecked 11.1.1954 on rocks on the West Side of Senja Island, north of the Lofoten Islands, Norway. All the crew were saved.

Lorella H455 and Roderigo H135: Lost 26.1.1955 ninety miles north east of the North Cape, Iceland. On 23.1.1955 *Roderigo* was steaming in company with *Lorella*, because *Lorella's* radar had broken down. Most ships were sheltering at Riker Huk but *Lorella* and *Roderigo* moved out to assist the *Kingston Garnet* who was caught in the bad weather with a fouled propeller, which she managed to free (24.1.1955) and reach shelter. The *Lorella* and *Roderigo* were now caught in severe gale force winds and freezing weather conditions, so they were unable to turn for shelter, and had to dodge into the wind on 26.1.1955. After fighting pitiless weather for three days, they were overwhelmed by the build up of ice and capsized. Forty crewmen were lost.

Stella Orion H379: Wrecked 7.11.1955 at Vestfjorden, North Norway, whilst homeward bound from the Barents Sea. All the crew were saved.

Prince Charles H249: Wrecked 23.12.1955. Ran aground on the Island of Socroeya 60 miles west of Hammerfest, during a snowstorm. The survivors were rescued from the shore, by the Norwegian ship *Ingoey* after two hours. Nine crewmen and one Norwegian pilot were lost. The wreck was salvaged and was towed back to Hull, where she arrived on 3.10.1956. She was repaired and became *Loch Melfort*.

St. Celestin H233: Lost 27.5.1956 after a collision with the Hull trawler *Arctic Viking* at Bear Island. Even though the sea was calm she sank within five minutes. All the crew were saved.

Staxton Wyke H479: Lost 23.8.1959, nine miles east of Hornsea. Whilst homeward bound from Iceland steaming in thick fog she was in collision with the 11,000 ton Newcastle ore-carrier *Dalhanna*. Almost cut in two she sank in under two minutes. Five crewmen were lost.

St. Hubert H142: Lost 29.8.1960 off North Norway, when a five foot cylinder which had been trawled up three days earlier and stowed to dump in deep water exploded; three of the crew were killed instantly and skipper Ness died later. The ship, her foredeck wrecked and hatches blown out had to run before a force eight gale, but after six hours she was abandoned and sank. The *Prince Charles* which had stood by her picked up the survivors.

Arctic Viking H452: Lost 18.10.1961 sixteen miles off Flamborough Head. She capsized in a severe gale whilst homeward bound. Survivors were picked up by the Polish lugger *Derkacz*; five crewmen were lost.

Stella Rigel H170: Wrecked 21.12.1962. Ran aground

near Toravaac lighthouse off the north coast of Norway whilst outward bound. Crew took to liferafts and were picked up by Norwegian fishing vessel *Siv*. All the crew were saved.

Kingston Turquoise H50: Wrecked 26.1.1965 on a sandbank about 14 miles NNW of Hoyhead, Orkney Islands. Although she managed to clear the sandbank the engine room crew found she was rapidly flooding and the crew abandoned ship. She sank; all this happened within a few minutes and one crewman was lost.

St. Romanus H223: Lost on or about 11.1.1968. Disappeared on passage to the Norwegian coast, during bad weather conditions. The mate of an Icelandic trawler reported he heard a May Day on 11.1.1968 and later a raft and lifebuoy were found; 20 crewmen were lost.

Kingston Peridot H591: Lost 26 or 27.1.1968. Probably capsized in bad weather conditions off North Iceland. She was heading home and had arranged on the 26th to rendezvous with *Kingston Sardius* on the Kiolsen Bank but she didn't arrive; 20 crewmen were lost.

Ross Cleveland H61: Lost 4.2.1968 whilst sheltering in Isafjordur in NW Iceland, three miles off Arnanes Light. Capsized and sank in exceptionally bad weather conditions; 18 crewman were lost, only one man was saved.

James Barrie H15: Wrecked 27.3.1969 on Louther Skerry, Pentland Firth, whilst outward bound for Iceland. Her crew was rescued by Wick lifeboat. On 29th at high tide she slid free of the reef and was taken in tow by two lobster boats and pumps put on board were operated by Kirkwall lifeboat crew. But she sank 1½ miles off Hoxa Head just 10 miles from where it was hoped to beach her. All the crew were saved.

Caesar H226: Wrecked 21.4.1971 at Arnanes at the entrance of Isafjord, whilst going into Isafjordur for repairs to the winch; all the crew were saved. She was refloated on 20.5.1971 but due to being badly damaged, she was towed out to sea to be sunk 300 miles off Iceland; but she sank prematurely, 39 miles off the Icelandic coast on 1.6.1971.

St. Chad H20: Wrecked 30.3.1973 at Ritur Huk at the entrance of Isafjord in a blizzard and severe gales, whilst sheltering with a large fleet of British trawlers. Her crew were picked up by the support ship *Othello*. All the crew were saved.

Ian Fleming H396: Wrecked 25.12.1973 off Havoysund 20 miles south-west of the North Cape whilst outward bound for the northerly grounds off Norway. She finally sank on 5.1.1974; 17 crewmen were saved but three were lost.

D. B. Finn H332: Grounded 21.3.1975 near Cape Hjorleifshofdi on Iceland's south coast, during hurricane force gales. All 21 crewmen were rescued. The *D. B. Finn* was refloated and returned to Hull. But it was decided she was too costly to repair and on 10.6.1975 she sailed for Blyth where she was scrapped.

The "Ross Cleveland". Lost 4th February 1968.

The "Kingston Peridot". Lost off Iceland 1968.

The "St. Chad". Wrecked at Riterhuk, Iceland, 30th March 1973.

THE SILVER COD CHALLENGE TROPHY 1954-1968

The Silver Cod Trophy was awarded from 1954 until 1968 by the British Trawler Federation to the Skipper and Crew of the trawler with the largest total catch for the year.

Year	Skipper	Vessel
1954	J. Hamling) R. Sackville-Bryant)	Arctic Warrior
1955	C. Taylor	Kirkella
1956	W. Turner	Lancella
1957	W. Lewis	Lord Beatty
1958	W. Lewis	Lord Beatty
1959	N. Longthorpe	Falstaff
1960	B. Wharam	Prince Charles
1961	C. Drever	Northella
1962	W. Brettell	Somerset Maugham
1963	R. Waller	Stella Leonis
1964	R. Waller	Stella Leonis
1965	W. Brettell	Somerset Maugham
1966	W. Brettell	Somerset Maugham
1967	W. Brettell	Somerset Maugham
1968	B. Wilson	Primella

		First	Second	Third
1954	**Vessel**	Arctic Warrior	Lorenzo	Caesar
	Skipper	J. Hamling R. S. Bryant	A. Ashcroft	W. Thompson
	Kits	42,776	41,735	39,680
	Days/£	332/£123,525		
1955	**Vessel**	Kirkella	Kingston Jacinth	Cape Spartel
	Skipper	C. Taylor	J. Shaugnessy	J. Woodell
	Kits	46,589	45,835	44,982
	Days/£	339/£129,563		
1956	**Vessel**	Lancella	Arctic Warrior	Kingston Jacinth
	Skipper	W. Turner	R. S. Bryant	J. Shaugnessy
	Kits	45,936	45,308	45,134
	Days/£	340/£131,633		

		First	Second	Third
1957	**Vessel**	Lord Beatty	St. Britwin	Portia
	Skipper	W. Lewis	J. Gibson	A. Ashcroft
	Kits	38,873	37,466	37,116
	Days/£	302/£114,927	£131,397	£129,806
1958	**Vessel**	Lord Beatty	St. Loman	Arctic Ranger
	Skipper	W. Lewis	J. Dobson	R. S. Bryant
	Kits	40,563	38,554	37,065
	Days/£	330/£155,903		
1959	**Vessel**	Falstaff	Arctic Ranger	Prince Charles
	Skipper	N. Longthorpe	R. S. Bryant	B. Wharam
	Kits	39,697	37,480	35,709
	Days/£	£134,263	£133,123	£135,640
1960	**Vessel**	Prince Charles	Falstaff	Northella
	Skipper	B. Wharam	N. Longthorpe	C. Drever
	Kits	39,603	38,787	36,822
	Days/£	346/£152,139	345/£147,816	345/£138,574
1961	**Vessel**	Northella	Cape Trafalgar	Westella
	Skipper	C. Drever	K. Neilson	W. Drever
	Kits	41,176	39,766	37,117
	Days/£	350/£162,062	332/£158,155	346/£163,177
1962	**Vessel**	Somerset Maugham	Falstaff	Northella
	Skipper	W. Brettel		
	Kits	46,557	40,165	40,155
	Days/£	351/£146,183	341/£124,208	344/£152,201
1963	**Vessel**	Stella Leonis	Somerset Maugham	D. B. Finn
	Skipper	R. Waller		
	Kits	39,556	37,998	33,795
	Days/£	335/£161,500	331/£137,224	338/£147,608
1964	**Vessel**	Stella Leonis	Somerset Maugham	Arctic Corsair
	Skipper	R. Waller		
	Kits	35,505	35,418	32,738
	Days/£	340/£144,503	337/£150,926	334/£143,511

		First	Second	Third
1965	Vessel	Somerset Maugham	Ross Leonis	Ross Canaveral
	Skipper	W. Brettel		
	Kits	37,669	35,784	34,172
	Days/£	326/£157,942	341/£149,454	347/£149,643
1966	Vessel	Somerset Maugham	Primella	Ross Leonis
	Skipper	W. Brettell		
	Kits	39,397	34,091	33,696
	Days/£	343/£165,655	336/£139,702	336/£138,553
1967	Vessel	Somerset Maugham	Arctic Brigand	Boston Concord
	Skipper	W. Brettell		
	Kits	39,247	38,561	35,088
	Days/£	339/£139,924	328/£134,482	330/£132,749
1968	Vessel	Primella	Ross Leonis	Ross Orion
	Skipper	Bill Wilson		
	Kits	40,844	40,192	39,806
	Days/£	348/£181,761	336/£170,938	337/£166,215

"Lord Beatty" won the Silver Cod in 1957 and 1958 with Skipper W. Lewis. She transferred to Grimsby in 1963 to sail with her German-built sister ships.

The crew of the "Lord Beatty" in 1958.

"Somerset Maugham" was the most successful Silver Cod winning trawler between 1962 and 1968. She won the trophy four times and was runner-up twice under Skipper W. Brettell.

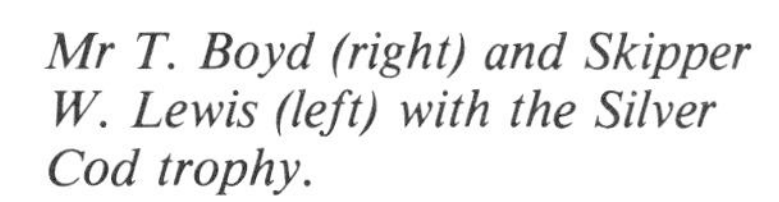

Mr T. Boyd (right) and Skipper W. Lewis (left) with the Silver Cod trophy.

H98 won the Silver Cod twice — in 1961 as "Northella" under Skipper C. Drever, and in 1968 as "Primella" under Skipper B. Wilson.

THE DISTANT WATER CHALLENGE SHIELD 1967-1977

The Hull Distant Water Challenge Shield was awarded from 1967 until 1977 to the Skipper and Crew of the trawler with the greatest value of catch for the year, on a points basis. These were calculated by adding the number of kits caught to the grossing in £'s and dividing by the registered speed of the vessel.

CHALLENGE SHIELD WINNERS

Year	Skipper	Vessel
1967	T. Thresh	Arctic Brigand
1968	B. Wilson	Primella
1969	D. Taylor/ W. Brettell	Somerset Maugham
1970	G. Boyce	Kingston Emerald
1971	G. Atherton/ J. Russell	Kingston Beryl
1972	J. Berry	Ross Trafalgar
1973	N. Beaves/ B. Ashcroft	Ross Altair
1974	W. Brettell	Hammond Innes*
1975	D. Taylor	Hammond Innes
1976	D. Taylor	C. S. Forester*
1977	D. Taylor	C. S. Forester

* The stern trawlers *Hammond Innes* and *C. S. Forester* were allowed to take part in the Challenge Shield Competition because they were freshers not freezers.

1967

Place	Vessel	Owner	Kits	Grossing (£)	Points
1	Arctic Brigand	Boyd Line	38,806.5	134,462.1	13,076.8
2	Kingston Sapphire	Hellyer/Associated	29,778.0	132,836.7	12,508.8
3	Ian Fleming	Boston Group	28,972.8	120,529.3	12,458.5
4	Ross Altair	Ross Group	31,180.3	129,518.7	12,361.4
5	Ross Orion	Ross Group	31,997.6	138,847.0	12,203.1
6	D. B. Finn	Boston Group	32,803.8	150,025.3	12,188.6

1968

Place	Vessel	Owner	Kits	Grossing (£)	Points
1	Primella	J. Marr & Son	40,383.6	181,743.1	15,866.1
2	Ross Sirius	Ross Group	39,569.0	159,376.0	15,303.4
3	Ian Fleming	Newington Trawlers	36,527.5	144,390.5	15,076.5
4	Ross Orion	Ross Group	39,873.2	166,208.3	14,720.1
5	Ross Leonis	Ross Group	42,018.2	170,908.8	14,684.6
6	Arctic Brigand	Boyd Line	36,570.7	155,611.3	14,504.3

1969

Place	Vessel	Owner	Kits	Grossing (£)	Points
1	Somerset Maugham	Newington Trawlers	43,662.0	210,106.0	17,204.6
2	St. Dominic	Hamling's	42,846.0	190,810.8	16,689.7
3	Westella	J. Marr & Son	38,742.3	202,234.8	16,619.1
4	Lorenzo	British United Trawlers	37,165.0	179,810.0	16,375.4
5	Ross Orion	British United Trawlers	41,798.1	186,128.7	16,280.4
6	Ross Canaveral	British United Trawlers	39,848.6	187,533.7	16,241.5

1970

Place	Vessel	Owner	Kits	Grossing (£)	Points
1	Kingston Emerald	British United Trawlers	36,526.9	232,682.7	20,317.7
2	Ross Canaveral	British United Trawlers	34,009.9	207,151.7	18,914.6
3	C. S. Forester	Newington Trawlers	35,039.0	220,853.0	18,278.0
4	Ross Orion	British United Trawlers	36,836.3	217,776.8	18,186.6
5	Macbeth	British United Trawlers	31,019.8	202,363.9	17,952.5
6	Arctic Ranger	Boyd Line	31,542.4	201,202.2	17,903.4

1971

Place	Vessel	Owner	Kits	Grossing (£)	Points
1	Kingston Beryl	British United Trawlers	31,108.7	260,416.5	21,594.4
2	Benvolio	British United Trawlers	31,206.4	242,508.8	21,467.8
3	Ian Fleming	Newington Trawlers	27,899.7	225,365.9	21,105.4
4	C. S. Forester	Newington Trawlers	32,196.7	262,904.7	21,078.6
5	Somerset Maugham	Newington Trawlers	33,450.6	272,668.2	20,753.8
6	Kingston Onyx	British United Trawlers	28,333.3	231,307.8	19,972.3

1972

Place	Vessel	Owner	Kits	Grossing (£)	Points
1	Ross Trafalgar	British United Trawlers	26,813.3	269,529.3	22,795.5
2	C. S. Forester	Newington Trawlers	31,576.8	266,983.7	21,325.7
3	Ross Altair	British United Trawlers	25,378.6	244,908.6	20,791.3
4	Ross Orion	British United Trawlers	26,426.2	250,836.1	19,804.4
5	Lorenzo	British United Trawlers	24,497.0	234,021.5	19,510.8
6	Loch Eriboll	British United Trawlers	24,405.4	231,426.0	19,308.0

1973

Place	Vessel	Owner	Kits	Grossing (£)	Points
1	Ross Altair	British United Trawlers	25,352.4	343,679.3	28,387.0
2	Westella	J. Marr & Son	26,984.5	379,473.0	28,031.5
3	Ian Fleming	Newington Trawlers	21,036.0	301,058.0	26,841.1
4	Arctic Vandal	Boyd Line	23,249.9	328,099.8	26,516.9
5	Arctic Ranger	Boyd Line	23,098.1	316,210.0	26,100.6
6	Kingston Onyx	British United Trawlers	23,090.2	312,832.1	25,840.1

1974

Place	Vessel	Owner	Kits	Grossing (£)	Points
1	Hammond Innes	Newington Trawlers	31,275.9	—	33,675.1
2	C. S. Forester	Newington Trawlers	31,810.6	—	32,360.7
3	Westella	J. Marr & Son	30,915.6	—	31,133.8
4	Ross Orion	British United Trawlers	28,637.4	—	30,712.1
5	Somerset Maugham	Newington Trawlers	28,732.1	—	29,955.2
6	Ross Leonis	British United Trawlers	29,863.4	—	29,811.9

1975

Place	Vessel	Owner	Kits	Grossing (£)	Points
1	Hammond Innes	Newington Trawlers	36,702.9	—	42,892.1
2	Ross Orion	British United Trawlers	33,066.3	—	37,217.9
3	Ross Canaveral	British United Trawlers	25,877.9	—	34,341.7
4	Somerset Maugham	Newington Trawlers	32,433.3	—	34,009.9
5	Lord St. Vincent	British United Trawlers	28,218.9	—	33,746.5
6	C. S. Forester	Newington Trawlers	29,246.8	—	33,633.6

1976

Place	Vessel	Owner	Kits	Grossing (£)	Points
1	C. S. Forester	Newington Trawlers	27,600.6	—	48,346.0
2	Hammond Innes	Newington Trawlers	27,950.5	—	47,351.2
3	Arctic Cavalier	Boyd Line	27,012.4	—	41,729.7
4	Somerset Maugham	Newington Trawlers	26,709.4	—	41,300.0
5	Ross Canaveral	British United Trawlers	23,674.3	—	39,957.2
6	Ross Sirius	British United Trawlers	21,732.9	—	39,832.6

1977

Place	Vessel	Owner	Kits	Grossing (£)	Points
1	C. S. Forester	Newington Trawlers	25,824.7	—	57,066.8
2	Ross Sirius	British United Trawlers	18,556.8	—	43,506.8
3	Somerset Maugham	Newington Trawlers	19,705.7	—	40,539.4
4	Arctic Cavalier	Boyd Lane	19,635.5	—	39,882.0
5	Loch Eriboll	British United Trawlers	17,419.4	—	38,543.7
6	St. Giles	Hamling's	16,745.6	—	38,215.7

The Challenge Shield winners, "Kingston Beryl" (1971) and "Ross Trafalgar" (1972), laid up in 1978.

The "Stella Altair", re-named the "Ross Altair" in 1965, won the Challenge Shield in 1973.

(Left) Commander Alan Ayres (left) with Mr Andrew Marr (centre) presenting the Challenge Shield to Skipper William Brettell (right).

(Below) The "Arctic Brigand" was the first Challenge Shield winner in 1967 with Skipper T. Thresh.

The "Loch Eriboll" at the Victoria Dock slipway in 1979.

LIST OF TRAWLERS SCRAPPED AT VICTORIA DOCK, HULL

In 1972 Albert Draper & Son Ltd., the Hull scrap-merchants, began renting the old slipways on the bank of the Humber at Victoria Dock, for shipbreaking purposes. Among the vessels which have been scrapped here were a number of trawlers from Hull, Grimsby, Aberdeen and Iceland.

Six Silver Cod winners ended their days here, along with Hull's first stern trawler, *Lord Nelson,* in September 1981.

The trawlers were stripped of all valuable equipment, towed to the slipway on the high tide, then allowed to settle on the mud. First the rails, masts, funnel and winches were removed, then the bow section; next the engine was removed and the engine-room flooded to act as a fire deterrent. To get rid of the wood and fittings in the accommodation and fishroom, controlled fires were started. While the hull cooled off, the stern section and propeller were removed. Next the bridge was removed as a whole unit. Finally, the lower section of the hull was towed round onto the cobbled slipway and cut into sections.

The job of cutting up the ships was tough work. The cutters wore heavy protective clothing with goggles, masks and hard hats to prevent the sparks from burning their eyes, skin and hair.

Weather-wise, the worst times of the year for the cutters were mid-summer, when the job was sweltering hot, and mid-winter, when everything froze.

FROM HULL	
Arctic Buccaneer	9.72
Calydon	6.73
St. Amant	6.73
Loch Inver	2.74
St. Apollo	5.74
Arctic Outlaw	9.3.74
St. Alcuin	24.6.74
Benvolio	2.3.75
Kingston Jade	26.4.75
Kingston Almandine	28.4.75
Newby Wyke	26.4.75
Arctic Ranger	26.10.76
Brucella	21.2.77
Primella	5.4.77
Ross Trafalgar	4.9.78
Somerset Maugham	19.9.78
Ross Leonis	4.11.78
Falstaff	31.1.79
Kingston Beryl	27.7.79
Loch Eriboll	9.10.79
Kingston Pearl	19.3.80
Joseph Conrad	15.8.80
St. Gerontius	11.10.80
Ross Sirius	7.4.81
Ross Altair	8.4.81
Arctic Viking	7.77
*Prince Charles	10.3.78
*William Wilberforce	23.5.78

FROM GRIMSBY	
*Lord Mountevans	11.73
Vanessa	4.75
*Lord Beatty	14.4.76
Northern Sky	14.4.76
Northern Eagle	8.76

FROM ABERDEEN	
Dinas	4.76
Arctic Invader	6.79
*Lucida	12.79
Partisan	13.4.83

FROM ICELAND	
Karlsefni	4.73
Arsaell Sigurdson	10.84
Jon Thurdason	10.84
Solbakur	10.84

* = Former Hull ships

(Above) An aerial view of St. Andrew's Dock. The dock was opened in 1883. The "Arctic Raider" was the last ship to leave it on 3rd November 1975. Photo by courtesy of Associated British Ports, Hull.

(Right) Albert Dock now serves the fishing industry. Photo by courtesy of Aerial Connections.

INDEX

Note: Each index entry refers to a ship's position in the main table only.